**WORLD RELIGIONS SERIES**
**Series Editor: W. Owen Cole**

# Buddhism

Peter and Holly Connolly

Stanley Thornes (Publishers) Ltd

First published in 1992 by:
Stanley Thornes (Publishers) Ltd
Old Station Drive
Leckhampton
CHELTENHAM GL53 0DN
England

British Library Cataloguing in Publication Data
Connolly, Peter
  Buddhism. – (World religions)
  I. Title    II. Connolly, Holly    III. Series
294.307

ISBN 1–871402-07-7

Typeset by Tech-Set, Gateshead, Tyne & Wear.
Printed and bound in Great Britain at The Bath Press, Avon.

# *Acknowledgements*

The authors and publishers are grateful to the following for permission to reproduce photographs:

Barnabys Picture Library, **pp. 15** and **29** • Benetton UK, **p. 3** • Jennie Bradshaw, **p. 93** • Chithurst Buddhist Monastery, **p. 126** • Circa Photo Library, **p. 43** • DLP Communications, **p. 4** • Diamond Information Centre, **p. 6** • Phil Emmett Pictures, **pp. 39, 51** and **81** (both) • Eye Ubiquitous/David Cumming, **p. 31** • Sally & Richard Greenhill/Alain Le Garsmeur, **p. 56** • Robert Harding Picture Library, **pp. 17** and **22** • Michael Holford, **p. 94** • Geoff Howard, **p. 130** • Hulton Picture Company, **p. 10** • Hutchison Library, **pp. 1, 20, 97** and **127** • Japan National Tourist Organisation, **pp. 73** (bottom right) and **106** • Manjushri Institute/Andy Weber, **pp. 71, 72, 74** and **76** • Mansell Collection, **p. 63** • Panos/Neil Cooper, **p. 131** • Ann & Bury Peerless, **pp. 42, 54, 73** (bottom left) and **80** (left) • David Rose, **pp. 45** and **125** • Vidocq Photo Library/Joan Batten, **p. 89** • Vidocq Photo Library/Julian Gearing, **pp. 80** (right) and **114** • Werner Forman Archive, **p. 133**.

The photo on **p. 73** (top) was supplied by the author.

Cover photos • top and bottom left, supplied by the authors • top right, Amaravati Buddhist Centre • bottom right, Circa Photo Library.

Extracts quoted in this book are taken from the following publications:

**p. 21** L. Stryk (ed.), *World of the Buddha* (Doubleday, 1968, pp. 146–7) • **pp. 43–4** E.J. Thomas, *The Life of Buddha as Legend and History* (RKP, 1949, pp. 65–6) • **p. 53** Nanamoli, *The Life of the Buddha* (Buddhist Publication Society, 1978, p. 318) • **p. 54** Nanamoli (op. cit., p. 335) • **pp. 61–3** E. Conze, *Buddhist Scriptures* (Penguin, 1959, pp. 146–9) (slightly adapted) reproduced by permission • **pp. 65–6** E.A. Burtt, *The Teachings of the Compassionate Buddha* (New American Library, 1955, pp. 142–4) (with minor changes) reproduced by permission • **pp. 67–8** E. Conze (op. cit., pp. 24–6) • **p. 75** E. Conze *et al.* (eds), *Buddhist Texts Through the Ages*, (p. 103)

Every effort has been made to contact copyright holders and we apologise if any have been overlooked.

# Contents

# A Note on Language

Buddhist scriptures have been preserved in many languages. In this book we have taken the Sanskrit version of words as standard when dealing with schools of Buddhism originating in India. When treating the Theravada school, the Pali equivalent of the Sanskrit word has been given as well, e.g. *karma* (Skt)/*kamma* (Pali). When dealing with far eastern and Himalayan forms of Buddhism, we have tended to use the terms from the relevant language (e.g. Japanese) but given Sanskrit equivalents where we thought it would be helpful.

## *Pronunciation*

Non-English words in the glossary are given with diacritical marks to aid correct pronunciation. The basic rules are:

vowels with a horizontal line above them are long ones (double the normal length)

| | |
|---|---|
| **ā** | is pronounced as 'aa' |
| **ī** | is pronounced as 'ee' |
| **ū** | is pronounced as 'oo' |
| **ō** }<br>**o** } | are pronounced as in roll |
| **e** | is pronounced as in prey |
| **c** | is pronounced as 'ch' |
| **th** | is pronounced as 't-h', not 'th' |
| **ph** | is pronounced as 'p-h', not 'ph' [f] |
| **ñ** | is pronounced as 'ny' |
| **ś** | is pronounced as 'sh' |
| **ṣ** | is pronounced as 'sh' |
| **ṃ** | is pronounced as 'n' (at the back of the mouth) |
| **ṇ** }<br>**ṭ** } | are pronounced with the tongue at the top of the mouth |
| **ḥ** | is pronounced as 'h' |

# *Introduction*

**?**

1. Have you ever wondered whether you will continue to exist after your death?
2. Have you ever wondered whether you existed before you were born?
3. Have you ever wondered why the universe exists at all?
4. Have you ever wondered whether some ways of behaving are always right and others always wrong?

Think about these questions for a minute and then write down your answers to them.

These questions are often thought about by religious people. The kinds of answers they give affect the way in which they think about themselves, their actions and the things which happen in the world.

For example, some people believe that they will be punished by God if they do something bad. If they fall off their bicycle they might understand this as the way God has chosen to punish them for some wrongdoing. So they try harder to be good. A person who does not hold the same belief might think of the fall as an accident or a result of lack of practice. So they decide to give more time to practising cycling.

This example shows us that if we want to understand why people behave in certain ways, we need to understand their beliefs about things. When a person studies religion, these two things – belief and behaviour – are looked at very carefully.

However, beliefs and ways of behaving change over time. So, to understand religion we have to look at the history of the beliefs and practices of whatever religion we are studying.

A person who studies religion is, first and foremost, studying people. In particular, they are studying what people believe and have believed about issues such as those listed at the beginning of this introduction. They are also studying how those beliefs affect and have affected the behaviour of religious people.

**?**

1   Write down your beliefs about the topics listed below and explain how they affect your behaviour:
   ● harming animals;
   ● stealing;
   ● drinking alcohol under age.

2   Think about someone who has beliefs which are different from your own (for example, they might believe in God whilst you do not, or vice versa).
   **a** Explain how their behaviour differs from yours because of the difference in your beliefs.
   **b** Perhaps their behaviour is no different from yours. They may do the same thing but for different reasons. Discuss reasons for vegetarianism or deciding not to have children as examples.

One thing which you will come to realise before too long is that even though religions have a lot in common there are also many differences between them. It is the differences between religions which are often the most difficult to explain. For example, if one religious person believes there is a God and another religious person believes there is not, which one is right?

As yet no one has worked out how to discover whether God exists. So we cannot answer the question of which believer is right. Does this mean that learning about religion is a waste of time? Not at all.

If our only reason for looking at religion was to work out which religions had 'true' beliefs and which had 'false' ones then we might not make much progress. If, on the other hand, we study religion so that we can better understand people, including ourselves, then there is a lot we can learn.

One of the things we can learn about ourselves is how we respond to people who have beliefs which are different from our own and who act in ways which we find difficult to understand.

## UNDER-STANDING DIFFERENCE

There are many different types of people living in the world. Some of the differences between yourself and people who live in other countries are easy to spot. They speak different languages, wear different kinds of clothes and their skin is often a different colour from your own.

**?**

1   Look at the picture. Have you ever been among a mixed group from different parts of the world, like the people in this picture?
2   Do you think there are many groups like this in Britain? If so, where?
3   How do you think the people in the picture feel about being together?

Your friends and classmates are different from you in many ways. There are even differences between yourself and other members of your family. Anyone who knows identical twins quite well can soon learn to tell them apart. The truth is that you are unique, there is no one else in the world quite like you.

**?**

1   Describe something about yourself which you think is unique.
2   How do you feel about being unique?
3   Have you ever wondered what it would be like to be someone else?

## DEALING WITH DIFFERENCE

Some people are a little bit different from you; others are very different. We all react to difference in a variety of ways.

**?**

Use the words in this box to help you answer the questions which follow:

| | | | |
|---|---|---|---|
| jealous | inferior | confused | happy |
| better | interested | amazed | |
| embarrassed | frightened | irritated | |
| awkward | angry | amused | |

1   How do you feel when you meet people who wear clothes which are very different from your own?

**2** How do you feel about people who live in houses which are very different from your own? For example, large or small, privately owned or rented, new or old, smart or scruffy?

**3** How do you feel when you meet people who behave differently from you? For example, alternative greetings or diets?

Mixing with people who are different from you might make you angry or upset. On the other hand, you may find it interesting and enjoyable. Some people avoid difference and only make friends with people who are similar to themselves. Other people like difference and often make friends with people who are not at all like themselves.

**1** Are your friends similar or different from you?
**2** How do those of your friends who are similar affect you?
**3** How do those friends who are different affect you?

## STEPPING INTO THE SHOES OF A BUDDHIST

*How do these feel?*

Do you remember ever dressing up as a child or pretending to be someone else, a hero or heroine perhaps? Actors and actresses do this all the time. When they pretend to be someone else they try to imagine what it would really be like to be that person. In their imagination, they 'step into the shoes' of the person they are pretending to be. An actress does not just move and speak like someone else, she tries to *feel* and *think* like the person she is imitating.

When we try to understand people who are different from ourselves, we need to imagine thinking and feeling like them. In this book, we are going to help you to understand how Buddhists think and feel. In our imaginations, we are going to 'step into the shoes' of a Buddhist. (We should remember, though, that even Buddhists are not all the same: in Thai villages many may go barefoot, but not in the streets of London.)

# Chapter 1

# *Three Basic Teachings*

Buddhism is a religion founded upon the teachings of a man who is referred to by the title 'Buddha', meaning 'Awakened One' or 'Enlightened One'. The Buddha lived in India 2500 years ago. People who believe in the teachings of the Buddha, and who base their lives on them, are called Buddhists. Buddhists say that these teachings have not dated or become old-fashioned, and that living now is not much different from being alive all those years ago. In other words, despite all the discoveries we have made and machines we have invented certain aspects of life and our basic reactions to living have not changed very much at all.

**?**

Look at these descriptions of feelings and actions. Write down any that you think may have been as true for someone living over 2000 years ago as they are for people today.

unhealthy and in pain
enjoying good food
lonely and all alone
rich and wealthy
not satisfied with life
proud of good looks

part of a family
poor and struggling
unhappy and depressed
healthy and fit
fed up with school
breaking rules

changing relationships
feeling successful
enjoying competition
happy and feeling good

The Buddha taught three things. Everything else that he said is based on these. They are:

● everything is always changing – impermanence;

● this means that we can never be happy with anything for very long – unsatisfactoriness;

● who 'I' am keeps changing – there is no such thing as 'the self'.

**IMPERMA-NENCE**

All living things are born and die. During their lifetimes they are always changing. Their hearts beat, they breathe, they digest food. Their cells are dying and being replaced all the time. We do not notice many of these changes if we see people or animals every day, but if we see someone only once a year we often notice a few things about them which are different. Even when we do not notice these changes, they are still taking place.

The same applies to the non-living world. Although rocks change more slowly than people or animals, they are constantly being worn away by water and wind. Eventually, even tall mountains become rolling hills.

Everything that we know of changes, and this process of change is happening all the time, from moment to moment. Even rocks change slightly every second of their existence.

*Diamonds are forever – fact or fiction?*

**?**

1   **a** Make two lists – one of things which change quickly and one of things which change slowly.
   **b** Was one list easier to write than the other?
2   Can you think of anything which does *not* change? Make a class list and discuss your answers.
3   Choose one item from your list of things which change quickly and use it to design a symbol which expresses nothing lasting forever – impermanence.

The Buddhist answer to the question 'Is there anything which does not change?' has three parts:

● if a thing has a beginning in time it cannot be permanent, it cannot last forever and must, in fact, be changing all the time;

- if a thing is made by other things or forces it cannot be permanent, it cannot last forever and must, in fact, be changing all the time;

- if a thing is made of parts it cannot be permanent, it cannot last forever and must, in fact, be changing all the time.

**?**

1  Can you think of anything which does not have a beginning?
2  Can you think of anything which is not made by other things or forces?
3  Can you think of anything which is not made of parts?

Discuss your answers.

The word used by Buddhists to refer to any thing, state or situation which has a beginning, is made up of parts, or is made by other things or forces is **conditioned**.

So the first teaching of Buddhism is that **all conditioned states are impermanent**, in other words, they do not last forever and, if you examine them closely, they are changing all the time.

This is the teaching of impermanence (*anitya*). Buddhists call this teaching 'the first mark or characteristic of existence'.

**?**

1  Write out in your own words what the Buddhist means when he or she says that all conditioned states are impermanent.

2  Write a discussion with a Buddhist giving your own views on this teaching and his or her response. It might be helpful to remember your class discussion when you write this.

# HAPPINESS AND UNHAPPINESS

*Everyone wants to be happy.*

1    What is happiness? Look up 'happiness' in a dictionary if you are not sure of its meaning.

2    What kinds of things make you happy? Make a list.

Think about the Buddhist teaching on impermanence. Now decide whether any of the items on your list of things which make you happy are permanent or do not change. Also, decide whether the happiness they give you is permanent or does not change.

Buddhists teach that not only do the things or experiences which make us happy change but also that the happiness we get from them changes too. That happiness either just fades away or is replaced by an experience which makes us unhappy. Our happiness is also impermanent.

Buddhists say that this is bad news. If all the things which make us happy, and even the happy feelings we have, are impermanent then our lives or our existence is not very satisfactory.

So the second teaching of Buddhism is that **all conditioned states are unsatisfactory**. This means we will never find lasting happiness if our happiness comes from or is based on anything which is impermanent. This is the teaching of unsatisfactoriness (*duhkha*).

Buddhists call this teaching 'the second mark or characteristic of existence'.

It sounds pretty grim. If everything which gives us happiness is impermanent then no matter how hard we try to set things up so that we can be happy in the future we will never succeed. We may be able to arrange things so that we get some happiness but we will never be able to avoid all unhappiness.

Because of this teaching, Buddhists are sometimes called pessimists, that is, people who always think and expect the worst, who always look on the dark side of things.

Buddhists, however, do not think of themselves as pessimists. Rather, they prefer the name 'realists'. They like to think of their way of looking at things as honest. They say that they do not want to hide from the truth. If the truth does not seem very nice, well that is just the way it is. It is no good trying to pretend that things are better than they really are.

1    If the truth about something is not very nice, do you think it is better to pretend that things are not really so bad or to face the truth realistically? Give reasons for your answer.

2    What sorts of things make you unhappy? Make a list.

3    Do you think animals can be unhappy? Make a list of the kinds of things which might make them unhappy.

4    Write out in your own words what a Buddhist means when he or she says that all conditioned states are unsatisfactory.

## THE PERMANENT AND THE HAPPY: NO-SELF AND *NIRVANA*

If Buddhists' understanding of things was based only on the first two teachings they might well become quite depressed. But they do not stop there. Buddhists add a third teaching to the first two. This is the teaching of no-self (*anatman*). It is usually put the following way: **all states are without self**.

Buddhists call this teaching 'the third mark or characteristic of existence'.

At this point two questions might have popped into your mind:

● what does the word 'self' mean?

● why has the word 'conditioned' been left out?

The answer to the first question is that 'self' (*atman*) means something like 'unchanging thing' or 'unchanging core' or 'unchanging essence' or 'unchanging substance'. In other words, for the Buddhist a 'self' is a kind of 'stuff' which does not change.

The answer to the second question is that Buddhists teach that there *is* a state which does not have the characteristics of the rest of existence. This state is an **unconditioned** state, a state which is not constantly changing, a state which is not unsatisfactory, for in that state there is complete happiness, complete contentment. This state the Buddhists call *nirvana*.

*Nirvana* is not an easy word to translate into English but you can think of it as the state where unhappiness has been put to an end. However, and this is an important point, *nirvana* does have one thing in common with the rest of existence, with conditioned states. This common feature is that, just like conditioned states, *nirvana* does not have a self and neither is it a self.

In other words, *nirvana* is not a 'stuff', neither is it a place.

*Nirvana* is simply that state or state of mind in which there is no unhappiness. Once this state of mind has been realised or attained it is permanent, a person cannot become unhappy again no matter what happens to them. *Nirvana* is the ending of unhappiness.

This is another reason why Buddhists do not think of themselves as pessimists. If there is an escape from unhappiness then we need not become depressed. Anyone who wants to be happy, and this includes most of us, can escape if they want to.

**?**

1  If *nirvana* is not a 'stuff' and not a place, then what can it be?
2  Imagine what a state like *nirvana*, where there is no discontentment, is like. Express this in a poem or a picture.
3  Write out in your own words what *nirvana* as an unconditioned state has in common with conditioned states.
4  Imagine that you are a Buddhist. Explain how your belief in *nirvana* stops you being depressed.
5  Write down the meanings of the following words:
   *anitya*      *duhkha*      *atman*      *anatman*      *nirvana*

<table>
<tr><td>

**Chapter 2**

</td><td>

# *Buddhist Teaching about the Individual*

</td></tr>
</table>

In their attempts to be completely honest about life, its pleasures and its pains, Buddhists cannot avoid the question 'What about *me*? Isn't there part of *me* that continues, even though my thoughts change from moment to moment and most cells in my body are replaced every seven years'?

*Which is the real me?*

1 Look at these three photographs of the same person. Do you think there is any part of them which stays the same?

2 Do you think part of you stays the same throughout your life?

Many people answer the second question with a 'Yes'. 'Yes there is part of me, the real me, which continues from moment to moment throughout my life.' Some people, however, have doubts about this answer.

Buddhists think that people and animals can be likened to flames. Although people and animals continue to exist for a period of time they, like flames, are just processes. Just as a flame is what happens when certain kinds of changes happen to wood or wax, so people are what happen when there are certain kinds of changes to food, air, sunlight and other elements.

**?** Explain in your own words the way in which Buddhists think that people and animal are similar to flames.

*More than the sum of its parts?*

Another way of thinking about the Buddhist way of understanding a person is to look at or imagine a bicycle. A bicycle is made up of parts: the frame, the wheels, the handlebars, mudguards, chain and so on. When one of these parts or components wears out we replace it with another. We can still recognise it as the same bicycle even though it is slightly different. Eventually, all the original parts might be replaced so that nothing of the original bicycle remains. However, because the change in parts has happened over a period of time we tend to think of it as the same bicycle – and in some ways it is. But, it is also true to say that in some ways it isn't.

For Buddhists, people are a bit like bicycles. They are made of parts. When some parts, such as cells, wear out, they are replaced. The continuity of the person, like the continuity of the bicycle, can be experienced even though most of its parts have been changed.

Discuss in class whether it is possible to draw a picture which expresses the Buddhist teaching about no-self.

## THE FIVE COMPONENTS (*SKHANDHA*)

### Component Number 1

In Buddhist teachings people are made up of parts or components (*skhandha*). The word *skhandha* literally means 'bundle' and this gives us the idea that the components themselves are made up of a number of smaller parts. According to Buddhism only one of the components is what we would call physical or material. The 'body', with all its parts, makes up 'the component of form' (*rupa skhandha*).

The other four components are what we would call 'mental'.

### Component Number 2

This is feeling, or sensation (*vedana*). For example, we have the experience of sight when our eye is stimulated by light and the experience of hearing when our ear is stimulated by sound.

We normally recognise five senses: sight, hearing, smell, taste and touch. Buddhists add one more. This sixth sense they call 'mind'. We experience this when the mind is stimulated by mental objects.

When we have any sense experience we normally decide very quickly what kind of experience it is. We classify it as pleasant or unpleasant, desirable or undesirable. Buddhists point out that the feeling or sensation is actually separate from the judgement about it. It is only the pure feeling that makes up 'the component of feeling' (*vedana skhandha*).

1   Try making a mental picture of an animal or person you know well. The experience of that mental picture is what the Buddhist would call a mind sensation or mind feeling.

2   Over the next day or two try to be aware of or take notice of as many of your feelings or sensations as you can. Watch how you decide whether they are pleasant or unpleasant. Do you think you have any choice in the decision?

### Component Number 3

This is perception (*samjna*). It is the part of us which decides whether a sensation is pleasant or unpleasant. It also makes sense of the pure feeling or sensation. To understand this let us consider an example. You might have a sensation of hearing. What you do not have at this point is an idea of what you are hearing. It could be anything. The ability to sort out one sound from another and decide 'that is the sound of an electric guitar' or 'that is the sound of a dog barking' is what the Buddhists call perception. It is this ability that Buddhists call 'the component of perception' (*samjna skhandha*).

Imagine you have landed on another planet where you do not recognise anything you see, hear or smell. Write a short story describing how you would feel and explaining how you would make sense of your experiences.

## Component Number 4

This is volition, or will, or intention (*samskara*). Components 2 and 3 deal with inputs, this component is responsible for outputs. This is the part of us which decides to do something, to say something or to think something. However, it is not entirely free in its activity. Take thoughts, for example.

Do you decide to think every thought that you think or do thoughts often appear on their own?
One way of checking this is to sit quietly for a time and stop thinking. If you find you can stop thinking just when you want to, then maybe your thoughts are all under your control. If, on the other hand, you cannot stop thinking when you want to, or if you find it difficult, this would suggest that your thoughts are at least partly independent of your will.

Buddhists think that our thoughts are affected by what we have thought, said and done in the past and also by what has happened to us in the past. So, our will is not completely free, it is affected by what has happened in the past. It is our conditioned will that Buddhists call *samskara skhandha*.

## Component Number 5

This is consciousness (*vijnana*). For the Buddhist there are six consciousnesses, one for each of the senses. The consciousness or awareness of sight or visual sensations is called visual consciousness. The consciousness or awareness of hearing or auditory sensations is called auditory consciousness, and so on through the six senses.

Match the senses listed below with their consciousnesses. You might want to look up some of the words in a dictionary.

| | |
|---|---|
| sight | auditory consciousness |
| hearing | visual consciousness |
| mind | olfactory consciousness |
| touch | gustatory consciousness |
| smell | tactile consciousness |
| taste | mental consciousness |

Taken together these consciousnesses make up 'the component of consciousness' (*vijnana skhandha*).

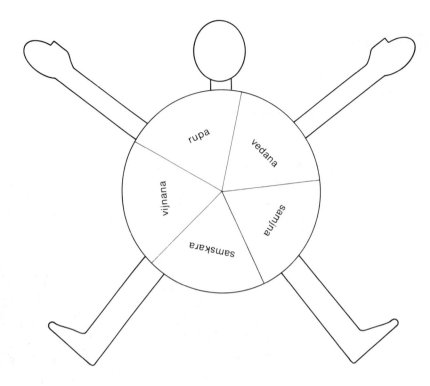

*The five components* (skhandha) *which make up a person according to Buddhism*

For Buddhists, these five components, or bundles of energy, make up a person. That's it! The lot! There is nothing else, no unchanging self. All of these components are constantly changing. You can identify them from one moment to the next just as you can identify a candle flame from one moment to the next. But, like the candle flame, a person does not have anything about them which does not change.

**?**

1    Match the words in the column on the left with their English translations in the column on the right.

| | |
|---|---|
| *skhandha* | sensation |
| *rupa* | perception |
| *vedana* | form |
| *samjna* | bundle |
| *samskara* | consciousness |
| *vijnana* | will |

2    Draw the diagram of the person (presented above) and write in the English translation for each of the parts.

3    What do you think about the Buddhist view of the person? Jot down your ideas on paper.

4    If you believed in the Buddhist description of a person, would it change the way you think about yourself? If so, in what ways would you change?

5    Why would a Buddhist say these changes were good?

Now discuss your answers to these questions.

# Chapter 3

# *Rebirth*

Most Buddhists believe in rebirth. That is, they think that they have had many lives before this one and, unless they attain *nirvana*, that they will have many more in the future. Buddhists also believe that their former lives have not all been as human beings. In fact, they think that, more often than not, they have been born as animals.

*Were you really my granny?*

**HUMAN OR ANIMAL?** The Buddha is reported to have said that getting a human birth is very difficult. The odds are against it since most of the life-forms on this planet (and elsewhere in the universe if there are extra-terrestrial life-forms) are non-human.

## The Giant Turtle

To help people understand how unlikely it is to be reborn as a human being, the Buddha gave the following example.

Imagine, he said, a giant turtle which lives on the bottom of the ocean. This turtle comes to the surface once every hundred years for air. Also, imagine a yoke (a kind of wooden life-ring) floating around on top of that ocean. The chances of being reborn as a human being are roughly the same as the chances that turtle has of putting its head through the yoke when it comes up for air.

## LIFE, DEATH AND REBIRTH

From the Buddhist point of view, if you want to go on being born again and again in animal and human forms nothing will stop you. That will happen automatically as a result of your desires. For Buddhists, death is not the end; we will always be reborn in another form unless we have attained *nirvana*.

You may have spotted something which seems odd here.

**?**

If people and animals do not have any permanent self what is it that is being reborn? Discuss your answers.

If we did have an unchanging self what would we mean if we said it was reborn? Would it know it was reborn? The answer must be 'No', for if the self really does not change it cannot know anything because knowing involves changing.

If we did have an unchanging self which was reborn would it be affected by being reborn in a different body? The answer again must be 'No'. If the self really is unchanging it cannot be affected in any way by anything that happens to any of its bodies.

So part of the Buddhist answer to the question of what is being reborn from life to life is that we cannot even make much sense of the idea that an unchanging self is being reborn since such a self cannot be affected by anything. What is more, if we ever came to 'know ourselves' it cannot be the unchanging self that is doing the knowing since, because it does not change, it cannot know anything.

Let us think back to the Buddhist description of a person (see Chapter 2). For the Buddhist, a person is made up of five bundles of energy, each of which is made up of smaller bundles. Death is just the breaking up of a particular arrangement of bundles. The smaller bundles which make up the body, the elements, go back to the universe at large. However, some of the 'mental' bundles stay together.

At this point we need to think again about the component of will (*samskara skhandha*) and the idea that many of our thoughts and actions are influenced by what we have done, said or thought in the past.

### Past and Present

How does the past affect the present? Part of the answer is 'through memory'. Some of our memories are conscious, that is we can bring them to mind at will. Other memories are unconscious, that is we cannot bring them to mind when we want to though they can be 'triggered' by unexpected events.

This brings us to an important question to which there is no straightforward, easily understood answer: 'how are our memories, both conscious and unconscious, stored?'

One thing which Buddhists say is that the energy from our past actions, words and thoughts is stored in a way that is similar to the way that memories are stored.

**?**

1    When you go home after school, have a look through some of your old things such as records, books or toys. Hold them, read them or play them and notice how they often help you to remember things which you do not ordinarily remember.

**2** **a** How much can you remember? Start with the present moment, the *now*. Close your eyes and start to remember everything that has happened in this lesson. Once you have done that, continue remembering all the way back to when you woke up this morning. Try to remember as much as you can.

    **b** Now discuss your memories with another person.

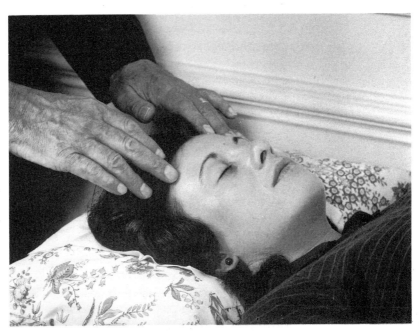

*Back beyond birth?*

Some people claim that, given the right conditions, we can remember in detail everything that has ever happened to us. Some also claim that under hypnosis people are not restricted to remembering events from their present life only, but can also remember events from previous lives.

## Actions – The Law of *Karma*

Buddhists think that it is the energy of our previous actions which keeps us being born in one body after another. However, not all actions produce this kind of energy. It is only voluntary acts that create after-effects which have to be worked out later in this life or in some future life.

This principle, that all voluntary acts have consequences which will have an effect at some time in the future, is often called the 'the law of *karma*'.

*Karma* is an old Sanskrit word which means 'act' or 'action'. In ordinary language it can refer to any action. When Buddhists talk about 'the law of *karma*' they are talking about the effects of voluntary actions.

The law of *karma* is often expressed in the following saying: 'As you sow, so shall you reap.' This means the kinds of experiences you have in your present life (what you reap) are determined by the kinds of actions you have done in the past (what you have sown).

Something you do today might bring its consequences tomorrow. Or you might not experience its consequences for many years.

**?**     If Buddhists believe in the law of *karma* can they also believe in injustice?

## LOOKING FOR A BODY

And so we come back to the question of rebirth. If a person dies, and they have the results of some past actions to be worked out or experienced, the energy or force of those results will find a way to express itself. In simple terms, it will create another body. Through this body the 'action-energies' or 'results of actions' can work themselves out.

However, the action-energy (*karma vipaka*) does not make another body by itself. It links up with the processes which are already taking place in the universe. For the making of a new human body it needs the help of a man and a woman.

The early Buddhists had a word for action-energy which is looking for a body – they called it the *gandharva*. According to Buddhist teaching, when the sperm of the man unites with the ovum of the woman a *gandharva* needs to be there for fertilisation to take place. No *gandharva*, no baby.

Of course the whole process is rather difficult to describe and the early Buddhists never did so in detail. What is clear though is that *gandharvas* are attracted to men and women whose situation, both physical and social, is appropriate for the kind of action–energy that makes up the *gandharva*. For example, if someone has been very cruel and has tortured many animals or people but has not had very many nasty things happen to them in their lifetime, then the *gandharva* of that person will be looking for a body that is going to get tortured and thereby suffer the consequences of their earlier bad actions.

The law of *karma* is not simply a one-to-one affair, though. Rather, the consequences of your actions get multiplied. The worse the actions, the more the consequences are multiplied. Actions which are just a little bit bad or just a little bit good are not multiplied very much.

Two other things to notice about the consequences of actions are:

- it is worse to kill big animals than it is to kill small ones;
- it is worse to kill holy people than it is to kill unholy ones.

The application of these principles means:

- it is more rewarding to help big animals than small ones;
- it is more rewarding to help holy people than unholy ones.

**?**     Arrange the following list of actions in the order of **best** (those producing the most good consequences) to **worst** (those producing the most bad consequences). Then discuss your lists.

bullying and hurting someone who is unpopular     killing a whale
feeding an unemployed, homeless person     killing an elephant
helping a friend with homework     killing a holy person

feeding a holy person
stealing from a shop
giving a home to a stray cat
hitting a dog with a stick

speaking out against injustice
being rude to your teacher
killing someone for money
killing a bird with a stone

## SAMSARA AND NIRVANA

So, for the Buddhist, the fact that all voluntary actions have consequences means that the bundles of matter and energy that we call 'ourselves' continue to exist life after life. There is not, however, any part of those bundles which can be called a true self, an unchanging part.

The process of rebirth which, according to Buddhists, has been going on from beginningless time is called *samsara*. It means 'wandering'. One of the main consequences of attaining *nirvana* is that *samsara* is brought to an end. A person who attains *nirvana* will not be born again.

**?**

Write down the meanings of the following words:
gandharva        samsara        karma        karma vipaka

## IN THE SHOES OF THE BUDDHIST

When we try, imaginatively, to step into someone else's shoes it is important to get some idea of the way they make sense of the world.

When a Buddhist reflects on or thinks about the world and the kinds of things people do, he (or she) uses the Buddha's teachings to understand what is going on. So, if he passes his exams he is pleased but he does not go 'over the top' because he knows that exam success is only a small part of happiness. Similarly, if he loses something of value he does not get too depressed for he believes that everything is changing and that he should not make his happiness depend on material things.

The Buddhist expects change to occur and is therefore not as upset as many people when major changes, such as a death in the family, actually take place. The Buddhist also believes that most of the things people do to get happiness are not going to work. He (or she) believes that even when people get a new car or new house or new stereo or new coat or new boyfriend/girlfriend they will still not be completely happy.

In fact, for the Buddhist, all this wanting things just makes the problem worse. For him, the way to get lasting happiness is to stop wanting things, and the way to do that is, first of all, to understand himself.

Once he can experience himself as five bundles of energy, rather than as a 'real', unchanging somebody, he can feel more comfortable in the world. He can feel more 'connected' to everything else, more a part of the flow and change that is existence.

We will look at how Buddhists go about this process of understanding themselves in the following chapter.

# Chapter 4

# The Four Noble Truths

The Buddha taught many people in many different ways. The most well-known version of his teaching, though, is the four noble truths.

## GETTING RID OF SUFFERING

'Two things do I teach', said the Buddha, 'suffering and its removal.' The four noble truths are the Buddha's more detailed version of this statement. The first two truths deal with the nature of suffering or unsatisfactoriness and its cause, whilst the third and fourth truths deal with the stopping of suffering and the way which leads to the stopping of suffering.

By putting his teaching in the form of the four noble truths the Buddha was informing people that he saw his task to be very similar to that of a doctor, namely healing the sick. The sickness which the Buddha sought to cure was the suffering or unsatisfactoriness which limits happiness in this life and will continue to do so in future lives.

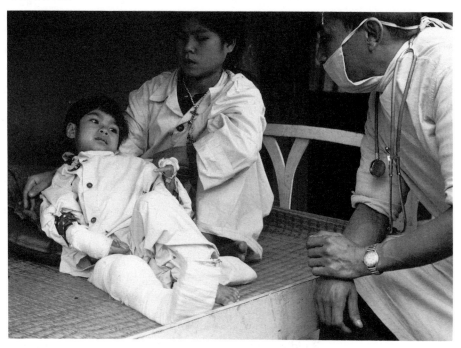

**?** Look at this photograph of a doctor – someone who, like the Buddha, heals the sick. Try to draw a picture of the Buddha's patients, suffering from the illness called 'the unsatisfactoriness of life'.

## No Answers to Some Questions

This approach of the Buddha's tells us that he was a very practical man. His main concern was to free people from suffering, and he used many methods for doing this. He did not, however, try to provide answers to certain questions which sometimes puzzled people if those answers did not help to get rid of suffering. So the Buddha did not provide answers to questions like 'Will the universe last forever?' and 'Does the soul exist after death?' Answering such questions would not help to get rid of suffering.

---

### *The wounded man*
In order to emphasise the practical nature of his teaching, the Buddha told a story:

> It is as if, Malunkyaputta, a man had been wounded by an arrow thickly smeared with poison, and his friends were to procure for him a physician or surgeon; and the sick man were to say, 'I will not have this arrow taken out until I have learnt whether the man who wounded me belonged to the warrior caste, or to the Brahman caste, or to the agricultural caste, or to the menial caste.'

> Or again he were to say, 'I will not have this arrow taken out until I have learnt the name of the man who wounded me, and to what clan he belongs.'

> Or again he were to say, 'I will not have this arrow taken out until I have learnt whether the man who wounded me was tall, or short, or of the middle height.'

> Or again he were to say, 'I will not have this arrow taken out until I have learnt whether the man who wounded me was black, or dusky, or of a yellow skin.' . . . That man would die, Malunkyaputta, without ever having learnt this.

---

1   The man in the story has a need to understand the situation he is in but he also has an arrow stuck in his body. What advice is the Buddha really giving him?
2   Make up a story of your own, based on life in Britain today, which makes the same point as that which the Buddha told.

The Buddha did not give answers to puzzling questions because he did not want people to be distracted from the more important task of getting rid of suffering. He also said that these types of questions were only asked by those who were confused in their understanding of themselves and life.

Think about the question, 'Does the soul exist after death?' If the Buddha had answered this question with a 'Yes', the questioner would have gone away thinking that he had a soul which was going to survive death. If, on the other hand, the Buddha answered it with a 'No', the questioner would have thought that he had a soul which was going to be destroyed at death. As far as the Buddha was concerned both answers are wrong. As we know from his teaching on no-self, the Buddha did not think that we had a self or soul whilst we are living, so to think of it as living on after death or being destroyed at death was just crazy and unhelpful.

Another example of a question which would only be asked by someone who is confused is 'Will dragons become extinct in the next 200 years?' The answer 'Yes' is wrong since it suggests that there are dragons now but there will not be in 200 years' time; the answer 'No' is wrong because it suggests that there are dragons now and that there will still be dragons in 200 years' time. The fact is, there are no dragons to become extinct anyway (at least most people think there are not).

**?**

1   **a** How would you respond to a person who asked you whether dragons will become extinct in the next 200 years?
    **b** What would you do if they also said 'answer yes or no'?
2   **a** Make a list of five questions which are sensible and five which are based on a confusion. Mix up the order.
    **b** Swap questions with someone else and see if you can work out which questions are sensible and which are confused.

## Finding a Cure for Suffering

When a doctor came to a patient's home in ancient India he would first of all work out what was wrong with the patient, in other words, he would diagnose the problem. This is what the Buddha did with the first noble truth. Then the doctor would explain what had caused the problem. This is what the Buddha did with the second noble truth. Thirdly, the doctor would say whether a cure was possible, which is what the Buddha did with the third noble truth. Finally, the doctor would suggest a cure or remedy if one was available. This is what the Buddha did with the fourth noble truth.

## THE FIRST NOBLE TRUTH

*Can anyone avoid suffering?*

In his first sermon (see Chapter 7) the Buddha spoke of the first noble truth of suffering or unsatisfactoriness (*duhkha*). He said,

> What then is the noble truth of suffering? Birth is suffering, decay is suffering, sickness is suffering, death is suffering. To be joined with what we do not like is suffering. To be separated from what we like is suffering. Not to get what we want is suffering. In sum, grasping at any [or all] of the bundles (*skhandha*) is suffering.

Although this sounds very gloomy the Buddha did not deny the existence of pleasure. What he did say, though, was that just like everything else pleasure was not permanent. As pleasure comes to an end, it is replaced by some degree of suffering.

At one end of the scale we have great pleasure being turned into great suffering. An example might be someone speeding along on a motorcycle on a summer's day: great fun. Then, change! The motorcycle hits a pothole, bounces out of control and the motorcyclist is smashed against a brick wall.

At the other end of the scale we have the slow and gradual lessening of pleasure. Getting a grade A for an assessment or eating a bar of chocolate gives a fair amount of pleasure. But, in every hour that passes after the experience of that pleasure it gets less. Eventually, we need another boost, or else we feel rather deprived or depressed. In the absence of pleasure we start to feel dissatisfied and to experience, even if only in a mild way, suffering.

**?**

1 Draw three pictures, one showing some kind of physical suffering, one showing some kind of mental suffering and one showing the kind of suffering which occurs when pleasure comes to an end.

2 **a** Think of three things that you enjoy doing – that give you pleasure. Get a friend to argue from a Buddhist point of view that they are not fully satisfying.

**b** Now you do the same with your friend's choices.

## THE SECOND NOBLE TRUTH

This concerns the arising (*samudaya*) of suffering. The Buddha said that the root cause of suffering is craving – wanting something so much that you feel you cannot be happy without it. If you have just got to have a new coat or go to a disco or have a date with a certain person and you do not get what you want, you suffer.

### Why Do We Want Things So Much?

Why do people get into the state of feeling that they need certain things to make them happy, why are they not content with things as they are?

The Buddha said that this was because people and animals do not understand what the world is really like, they are ignorant, they lack a knowledge of the way things are. Because they lack this knowledge, people seek their happiness in ways that will eventually lead them to experience more suffering.

People who do not understand what the world is really like are a bit like people wearing blindfolds. In other words, they make mistakes and they bump into things. For example, a person who wears a blindfold might take a path because it is flat, thinking that he or she will be happier or safer on flat ground. If, however, the flat ground leads to a swamp they are just walking into trouble without knowing it. The hilly path, although it might seem more difficult, could be the one which leads to safety. The right decision can only be made if a person takes off the blindfold or is guided by someone else who has been able to take off their blindfold.

So, from the Buddhist point of view, not understanding the way the world works makes people want things that they might not get or which will lead them into more suffering.

**1**   Write down five words which describe what wanting something feels like. Is it a pleasant or an unpleasant feeling?

**2**   List three things you have really wanted at some time in your life; then answer the following questions from a Buddhist standpoint:

**a**  did you ever have any of the things you wanted so much?

**b**  did having any of them make you happy? If so, how long did the feelings of happiness last?

Discuss your answers.

## Wanting Things Causes Rebirth

When people go after things they want, their thoughts and actions all create consequences. These consequences later cause them to be reborn into another body and the whole process starts all over again.

The Buddha called this sequence or pattern of events **dependent origination** (*pratitya samutpada*). For Buddhists this is a very important teaching. When you put the teachings of no-self and dependent origination together, you get a teaching that is found only in Buddhism. It is a teaching which makes Buddhism distinctive and different from other religions.

Dependent origination can be thought of in two ways, in terms of time and in terms of space.

### The past affects the present

In terms of time, dependent origination means that nothing comes into being or starts to exist on its own. Everything which comes into existence does so because of something that happened before. In other words, everything that exists now is connected with and influenced by what has happened in the past. It is a bit like a row of dominoes standing next to each other. If one gets knocked over it knocks the next one over and that knocks the next one over and so on. The main difference is that, as far as Buddhists are concerned, the process has been going on for as long as we can imagine and will continue into the future for as long as we can imagine unless, of course, we attain *nirvana*.

Find two key sentences from the passage above which describe dependent origination from the point of view of time. Write these down.

### Nothing is separate from anything else

In terms of space, the teaching of dependent origination means that all the people and things we see and hear and feel around us are not really separate from the rest of what is going on.

Human beings are in a constant state of exchange with the environment in which they live. The most obvious example of this is breathing. We are constantly taking in air, extracting the oxygen and breathing out the rest, adding some carbon dioxide as we do so. Plants work the opposite way. They breathe in carbon dioxide and breathe out oxygen. Without plants we would not be able to exist. Our existence is dependent on the existence of plants (and of animals too). It is also dependent on the existence of water and heat (the sun). Without these things we would not exist. Our existence is dependent on their existence.

Another way of putting this is to say that we are not self-contained beings. We do not have boundaries through which nothing passes, where nothing gets in and nothing gets out. Our boundaries are flexible, are permeable. They allow a two-way traffic: we take in what we need, we give out what we do not need.

Scientists sometimes talk about 'the web of life'. Let us think about a web or a net for a moment. From one point of view a net can be said to be made up of a certain number of squares. But how accurate is this way of describing it?

**?**

1    Look at this picture of a net. It has 64 squares. Copy it in pencil.

2    Now rub out one of the squares from near the middle and draw it on another piece of paper; or, if you have a string net, cut out the square and place it on the table.

3    How many squares have you got left? Write down your answer and then check it against the answer at the bottom of the page.

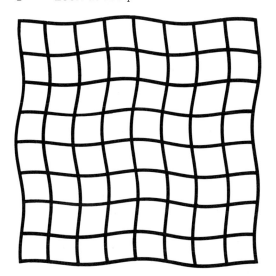

What this example shows is that the way of thinking about the net as being made up of 64 individual squares is a mistaken one. Each of the squares is dependent on the others for its existence.

According to Buddhists, the same thing applies to us. If we think of ourselves as separate from everything and everyone else, we are making a big mistake. The truth is that we are connected with everything and everyone else.

*Answer* – 55. The net had 64 squares but if you cut out one of the middle ones you destroy eight others as well. So, in this example, 64 − 1 = 55.

## THE THIRD NOBLE TRUTH

Once a doctor has worked out the cause of an illness he or she has to decide whether a cure is possible. When the Buddha came to understand the cause of suffering he knew that suffering could be removed. The third noble truth is the removal (*nirodha*) of suffering. So, from the Buddhist point of view, we do not have to be stuck with suffering.

Like everything else that has a cause, suffering is impermanent. As long as people do not understand the way things are, they will create more and more suffering for themselves. But once they know what the world is really like, once they are able to take their blindfold off, they become free to avoid the kinds of thoughts, words and actions which create suffering.

### An Optimistic View

It is because they think that suffering can be removed that Buddhists would describe themselves as optimists rather than pessimists. There is also another reason for Buddhists thinking of themselves as optimists. Not only do they think that suffering can be got rid of, they also claim to have the method for doing it.

**?**

1    Explain in your own words what is optimistic about the Buddhist third noble truth.
2    Write down the English equivalents of the following words:
    *duhkha*        *samudaya*        *pratitya samutpada*        *nirodha*

## THE FOURTH NOBLE TRUTH

The fourth noble truth is the path which leads to the removal of suffering. In the early Buddhist scriptures it is called **the noble eightfold path**. In some of these scriptures it is made clear that step 2 follows step 1, step 3 follows step 2 and so on. But some modern Buddhists say that the path should not be understood in this way at all. They teach that, as far as a person is able, he or she should practise all eight steps or parts of the path at the same time.

### The Umbrella Image

An image which modern Buddhists often use to help people understand their view of the path is that of an umbrella. An umbrella has eight spokes and each one can be taken as representing one of the parts of the eightfold path. The person who is not following the eightfold path is like someone on the outside edge, the circumference of the umbrella. They go round and round and round, just like the beings who are in *samsara* go round and round and round on the wheel of rebirth.

The person who is on the eightfold path, however, is moving along the spokes towards the centre – which represents *nirvana*.

**?**

Using the information from the top of p. 27, draw two pictures, one showing the eightfold path as a step-by-step journey to *nirvana*; the other showing it as the practice of all eight parts at the same time.

## The Eight Steps

Whether Buddhists think the eight steps should be followed in order or practised at the same time, the steps themselves are always the same:

1 right view;
2 right intention;
3 right speech;
4 right action;

5 right livelihood;
6 right effort;
7 right mindfulness or recollection;
8 right concentration.

In some texts a tenfold path is mentioned. The last two steps are right knowledge and right release.

## Right View

Right view has two main features. Firstly, it is a direct experience of the four noble truths. It is a vision of the world being full of suffering; it is a vision of the cause or origin of suffering; it is a vision of the fact that suffering can be brought to an end; it is a vision of the path which leads to the ending of suffering. This is why right view is always put first in the list of the eight parts of the path.

This vision is not something that someone else tells you about, it is something you experience yourself.

The second feature of right view is the effect it has on a person. A major result of having this vision is that most of the stored-up consequences of past actions are destroyed. These stored-up consequences affect people in many ways. They influence the family a person is born into and the kinds of qualities a person has. They also affect the way a person understands things and how they act.

In one way or another the stored-up consequences of past actions limit a person's freedom much as a habit, such as smoking, can limit someone's behaviour. In particular they can limit a person's freedom to follow the eightfold path and to put its recommendations into practice. So if a person is going to be successful in following the eightfold path it is helpful, if not essential, to be as free as possible from the effects of past actions. This is another reason why right view always comes first in the list of the parts of the eightfold path.

1  How do habits influence people's behaviour and limit their freedom?
2  Think of something you have done in the past, the effects of which you can still feel strongly. Describe what you did and how it affects you now.

### *Obtaining right view*

During the time of the Buddha most people experienced right view whilst listening to him preach a sermon. This was partly because the Buddha was a very skilful teacher. He knew exactly how to put things to help someone understand his teaching. It was also partly because many of the Buddha's early followers were at that point in their spiritual development where they were ready to understand what he had to say. Nowadays Buddhists have to work much harder to get right view. Many of them do as many good works as possible so that in this or some future life they will be able to hear Maitreya, the future Buddha (see Chapter 11), preach on the four noble truths.

1    Write out, in your own words, what it is that a person 'sees' when he or she obtains right view.
2    How might Buddhists in Britain today try to obtain right view?

## Right Intention

Once a person knows where they are going they can begin their journey. Once a Buddhist has experienced right view he or she can begin to progress along the path which leads to *nirvana*. The practice of meditation required by steps 6, 7 and 8 of the path can only be successful if it is based on a solid foundation of good or moral behaviour. Moral behaviour involves thoughts, words and deeds. A person's thoughts affect the words they speak and the deeds they do. So the second step of the eightfold path focuses on the kinds of thoughts or intentions a person has.

### *What are the right kinds of thoughts?*
The Buddha said that the right kinds of thoughts to have were those which had the qualities of non-harming, good will and renunciation, which means the giving up of worldly desires such as greed or power.

1    List three feelings that most people have which might make it difficult for a Buddhist to have the right kinds of thoughts. Try to explain why they might make it difficult.
2    Can you remember a situation where your intentions or thoughts were to hurt someone or wish them ill or to possess something which belonged to someone else? Share your recollections with a friend and discuss how those thoughts or intentions made you feel.
3    How might a Buddhist encourage you to deal with such feelings?

## Right Speech

The third step of the path deals with the way we use words. The Buddha encouraged his followers to avoid all kinds of hurtful and harmful speech. When giving advice to a young priest, the Buddha said that his disciples abstained from lying, slander, harsh language and vain conversation; neither did they repeat what someone else had told them in order to start a quarrel or to create bad feeling somewhere else.

Instead, the Buddha recommended that his followers speak in a positive way. He said that they should tell the truth, encourage people to be friends and to live peacefully.

1    Do you think that telling the truth is always a good thing? Write down the reasons for your answer.
2    Which do you think is worse, swearing or hurtful speech? Discuss your answers.
3    What would be the Buddhist answer to these questions?

### Right Action

The fourth step of the path deals with the way people act.

*No killing*

When he gave advice to the young priest the Buddha also said that his disciples did not kill living beings. Rather, they are kind to all living beings. There is a story about this:

> Once, in the high mountains of Tibet, lived a Buddhist monk who did not have a dog to walk each morning. Instead, when he got out of bed he would walk down to a pool among the rocks where a large old fish lived. When the monk arrived the fish would come out of its resting place and let the monk stroke it.

1   Do you think this story is true? Discuss your answers.
2   Why do you think animals trust some people more than others?

As they do not want to harm any living beings, many Buddhists are vegetarian – they will not eat meat.

1   How do you feel when you see a display of meat as shown in this photograph? Write down five words which express your feelings.
2   List as many reasons as you can for and against vegetarianism. What arguments would Buddhists give?

*No stealing*

The Buddha also said to the young priest that his disciples did not take anything which was not given. This means that Buddhists should not steal; nor should they keep anything they find.

Taking something not given includes various forms of trickery such as using false weights, fraud, insider dealing on the stock market and using public money for personal gain.

Think about the relationship between what Buddhists call right action and the law. To a Buddhist, can an action be
**a** legal and yet wrong?
**b** illegal and yet right?
List some examples if you can think of any and discuss your answers.

### No sex outside marriage

In some parts of his teaching the Buddha set down different standards of right action for monks and nuns and for lay people. Sexuality is one area where the Buddha made such a distinction.

Buddhist monks and nuns are not allowed to engage in any sexual activity whatsoever, they are not even allowed to touch each other. Things are less strict for lay people. They may engage in sexual intercourse, but only with their husbands or wives.

From the Buddhist point of view, sexual desire (*kama*) is one of the strongest forces which bind beings to the round of rebirth. So, unless a person can reduce their sexual desire they cannot make much progress towards the attainment of *nirvana*.

The Buddhist rules, or precepts, concerning sexual activity help people to reduce their sexual desire in various ways. Techniques such as meditating on the rotting corpse of a person of the opposite sex are sometimes used. This particular exercise was mainly for monks and nuns and is rarely practised today. For most lay people the effects of imagining the rotting corpse of a person of the opposite sex would be powerful enough.

### Acting positively

Just as right speech involves both what to avoid and what to do, so too does right action. Instead of wanting to harm beings Buddhists cultivate lovingkindness towards them; instead of wanting to steal from others they try to cultivate generosity; instead of indulging sexual appetites they cultivate restraint and tranquillity of mind.

List three ways in which meditating on the rotting corpse of a person of the opposite sex might help to make men or women considerably less attractive to you.

## Right Livelihood

Buddhist lay people are required to avoid earning a living in any of the following ways:

- dealing in weapons;
- dealing in living beings;
- dealing in flesh (meat);
- dealing in intoxicants;
- dealing in poisons.

They are also discouraged from engaging in lending money to gain interest (usury).

Monks in the Theravada tradition of Buddhism (see Chapters 10 and 15) are not allowed to handle money at all in case they develop a liking for money itself or for the way it might help them to manipulate other people.

1   Why do you think Buddhists are required to avoid earning a living in the ways mentioned above? Make a list.

2   **a** List the following occupations under (i) acceptable to Buddhists and (ii) unacceptable to Buddhists. Then compare your list with someone else's.

| | |
|---|---|
| cook | engineer |
| teacher | butcher |
| soldier | carpenter |
| banker | doctor |
| carpet fitter | nuclear power worker |
| pet shop owner | fisherman |
| police officer | lawyer |
| publican | tobacconist |

**b** Discuss the reasons for your selection.

3   Write a story about being an unemployed Buddhist at the Job Centre.

## Right Effort

The sixth step of the path, right effort, is about an activity which Buddhists call meditation.

*A Buddhist meditating*

Meditation works on the mind. Its purpose is to remove unwholesome, unhelpful states of mind, replacing them with wholesome, helpful ones. A mind which is full of strong feelings like anger, lust, greed or hatred twists the way a person understands what is happening in the world. A person with such a mind is often locked into just one way of seeing things.

For example, someone who hates another person always sees the other's actions as bad. Even if the other person acts generously the hate-filled person will think that the generosity is false and that the person only acts in that way to make people like him or her. The hate-filled person is therefore blinded to some parts of reality.

On the other hand, a person whose mind is free from these feelings, who is tranquil, generous and open to others, is much more likely to have a better understanding of things. This, in turn, leads to better decisions and more skilful kinds of behaviour.

## Removing and replacing

When a Buddhist is encouraged to practise right effort he or she is given guidance on how, through meditation, to remove unwholesome states of mind and then to prevent new unwholesome ones from arising. He or she is also taught how to maintain wholesome states of mind and to develop new ones.

- To **remove** unwholesome states of mind, a person can replace them with wholesome ones. For example, if they are thinking nasty thoughts about someone they can change them into nice ones.

- To **prevent** unwholesome states of mind from arising, meditators can turn their attention to something else or change the unwholesome states of mind into wholesome ones before they become habits.

- To **maintain** wholesome states of mind, a meditator can think about the benefits that come from feeling nice about other people, such as having lots of friends and smiling and laughing easily.

- To **develop** wholesome states of mind there are a number of practices a Buddhist can use. One of these is called the Brahma Viharas (sublime states).

## The Brahma Viharas

This is a practice where the meditator tries to cultivate four wholesome states of mind:

- the state of feeling **lovingkindness**, which is gentle and tender;

- the state of feeling **compassion**, which is an understanding and concern for those who suffer;

- the state of feeling **sympathetic joy**, which is gladness and pleasure when something goes well for another person;

- the state of feeling **equanimity**, where the mind is not ruffled or agitated but calm and balanced.

The Buddha encouraged his followers to develop these qualities one at a time in the following way:

*Start* by directing the quality towards yourself. So, if you are developing lovingkindness, direct it towards yourself, love yourself, feel tender towards yourself. *When* you know what it feels like, direct those feelings towards a person who has helped you in your search for happiness, a meditation teacher for example. *Then* direct the feeling towards a close friend; *next*, direct the feeling towards a neutral person, perhaps someone you hardly know, a bus driver or milkman for example. *Then* direct the feeling towards a person who does not like you or whom you do not like. *Finally*, direct the feeling all around you in every direction, to all points of the compass, upwards and downwards. Fill the entire universe with the quality you are working with. Let it soak into all living beings and benefit them.

1  Summarise in your own words the aim of practising right effort.
2  List four key words which guide the practice of right effort.
3  What do the words 'Brahma Vihara' mean?
4  What four qualities are cultivated by someone who practises the Brahma Viharas? Describe each of them.

## Right Mindfulness or Recollection

The seventh step of the path is about mindfulness and recollection. Right recollection is remembering past experiences. For most of us our memories are quite limited. If we think back over the last year only a few events will come immediately to mind and even then we might not remember them in the right order.

Sit quietly and try to recollect everything you have experienced during the last week. How easy did you find it?

Part of the practice of right recollection is learning how to bring experiences to mind so that we come to understand who we are, what we are and how the various events in our lives are connected together.

*Being aware*
Right mindfulness is also bringing to mind or being aware of what is happening right now in the present moment.

Buddhists are taught to start by training themselves to be aware of their breathing. They practise meditation exercises which require them to sit still, close their eyes and watch the rhythm of their breathing. This sounds simple but is very hard to do because most people's minds drift very easily. Each time their attention wanders, Buddhists are told to let their minds go gently back to watching the breath. Through practice this becomes easier to do.

Buddhists also practise being mindful of other bodily characteristics and activities such as posture and sensations. More advanced meditators learn how to be aware of subtle and quickly-changing events such as thoughts and feelings.

1  How aware are you? In pairs, tell each other about how you have been breathing, how you have been sitting and how you have been feeling in the last half-hour.
2  Are you aware of what you have been thinking since you started the previous activity? Write down all the thoughts you can remember or draw pictures of all your thoughts.

## Right Concentration

The eighth step of the path is about concentration. Before a Buddhist can experience awakening or enlightenment he or she has to learn to concentrate.

### *Flashlight to laser beam*

Concentration is very difficult for most people. Just think about your own experiences of trying to concentrate when reading a difficult book or even simply trying to concentrate on what your teacher is saying for a whole lesson.

Even when you do concentrate on something, lots of other thoughts pass through your mind as well. For 'right concentration' a person needs to be able to bring their mind to a state of perfect stillness. Ordinary people's minds are rather like the beam of a flashlight. The light spreads out very quickly and we cannot see very much with it. A concentrated mind is more like a searchlight, and a mind which has reached right concentration is like a laser beam.

**?** Focus your attention on one thing, a pencil, a book or an image in your mind. Keep your attention on it for as long as possible. No other thoughts, images or objects should enter or pass through your mind. How long can you do it for?

### *How Buddhists learn to concentrate*

Turning your mind into a mental laser beam takes a lot of practice, so Buddhists have developed many techniques to help people learn how to concentrate. For example, a meditator can concentrate on a dish of water and then, when they have it firmly fixed in their mind, close their eyes and see an image of it in their 'mind's eye'. Then they learn how to hold the image in their mind for a long period of time.

### *The Buddha's concentration led to understanding and enlightenment*

When a person's mind is perfectly concentrated, when it is like a mental laser beam, it can be focused directly on to the nature of things.

On the night of his enlightenment (see Chapter 6), the Buddha brought his mind into a state of perfect concentration. In the first part of the night, he used his concentration to remember all of his former lives. This enabled him to understand how he came to be where he was and how his actions in one life influenced his situation in another.

In the second part of the night, the Buddha used his concentrated mind to focus on the lives of other beings. He saw that their experiences in one life were affected by what they had done in former lives.

Finally, in the third part of the night, the Buddha turned his concentrated mind inwards in order to destroy the habits and desires which had kept him trapped in the round of rebirth.

**?** Write out in your own words what the Buddha did on the night of his enlightenment.

What the Buddha came to understand when he turned his concentrated mind inwards during the third part of the night was that three very deeply rooted habits or patterns were responsible for keeping beings trapped in the round of rebirth:

- sexual desire;

- desire to preserve individuality;

- ignorance of the true nature of things.

**?**

Think about any television programmes you have seen about wild animals. What kinds of things do you see them doing? Make a class list.

You probably all agreed that animals spend a lot of time obtaining food and protecting themselves from danger. These are two of their regular activities. Other regular activities are mating and caring for offspring. It is these instincts or drives which force animals – including humans – into the kind of behaviour which keeps them trapped in the round of rebirth. It was these drives which the Buddha uprooted when he became enlightened.

- **Sexual desire limits understanding**  As long as a person experiences the strong sexual feelings that all animals have, their understanding is distorted or obscured. Sexual desire leads to patterns of thought and action which Buddhists say create consequences which, in turn, hold beings in the round of rebirth.

- **Preserving individuality limits understanding**  Most people value their individual welfare too much. They are prepared to let others starve so that they can have more things, bigger houses and expensive holidays. From the Buddhist point of view, this attitude and this kind of behaviour is not based on correct understanding. No one can live without a supportive environment. We breathe, eat food and form relationships with others. When a person dies life carries on. No one is so important that others should suffer so that they can pamper themselves with luxuries. Yet many people think that their own welfare is the most important thing there is. This way of thinking prevents them from feeling connected to the rest of existence.

- **Ignorance limits understanding**  The third limitation on understanding which the Buddha learned to overcome is ignorance, that is the tendency we all have to misunderstand what the world is really like.

We have this tendency because of the way in which our brains deal with the information provided by our senses. First of all, our senses are selective. Human beings are only aware of light and sound waves within certain frequencies, for example. Dogs can hear sounds we cannot hear and some reptiles can see infra-red light we cannot see.

The information which our senses can pick up is generally organised according to principles which are learned from other people, mostly our families and people from our immediate society or culture. For example, some cultures teach that it is wrong for women to show their bodies in public. Women in these cultures are taught to cover themselves almost completely. In contrast, other cultures teach that it is fine for women to wear very little clothing. These cultural value-judgements strongly affect the experiences of people who accept them.

Individuals also see the world in different ways according to their personal beliefs and attitudes. For example, an old person who likes young people might see a group of teenagers who were laughing, shouting and chasing each other around in a very positive way. Another old person who does not like young people might see the same group of teenagers as noisy and irritating. In short, the way people understand the world is powerfully influenced by the beliefs and attitudes they bring to their experience of it. To project on to the world views which do not correspond to the way it really is, is what the Buddha called ignorance.

**?**

1    Think of someone you know who has a very strong feeling or a rigid attitude towards something. Write a description of what they feel strongly about and explain how it might limit their understanding.

2    What do Buddhists mean by 'ignorance'?

3    What would Buddhists say is the harm in ignorance?

## Right Knowledge and Right Release

Once the Buddha got rid of ignorance he realised that what he had just done had freed him from the need to be reborn. He also realised that he would not have to suffer any more. He might experience pain, of course, but that would not make him suffer because, since he understood everything clearly, he was able to accept pain as part of life. He became non-ignorant and no longer compelled to behave in ways that animals and other humans do. He became enlightened, he became a *buddha*.

The understanding obtained by the Buddha of his own past lives, of the reasons why people are born into different situations and of the factors which limited his understanding and freedom is called, in the Buddhist scriptures, 'right knowledge'. In some texts it is described as the ninth step of the path.

The freedom from suffering and rebirth which comes with that understanding is called 'right release'. This is sometimes referred to as the tenth and final step on the path.

## Part II  EARLY BUDDHIST SCRIPTURES AND THE LIFE OF THE BUDDHA

<table>
<tr><td>

**Chapter**

**5**

</td><td>

# *The Pali Canon*

</td></tr>
</table>

The Buddhist scriptures were composed over a long period of time. Many of them were remembered and passed on orally for many generations before they were written down. During this time, certain texts had parts added to them. Some texts were composed long after the Buddha's death (traditionally 483 BCE), but even so were considered by later Buddhists as scriptures.

Generally, the Buddhist scriptures were written by monks and nuns as a way of preserving the teachings of the Buddha. They were not written by historians for historical reasons. What this means is that although the scriptures contain a lot of information about the Buddha and his teachings, it is not all of the same kind.

**THE EARLIEST BUDDHIST SCRIPTURES**

The Theravada (Way of the Elders) school of Buddhism has preserved the oldest existing collection of Buddhist scriptures. It is called the Pali Canon since it is written in an ancient Indian language called Pali.

The Pali Canon is divided into three parts, each of which is further subdivided into smaller parts. Each of the three main parts is called a basket (*pitaka*), probably because the palm leaves on which the scriptures were written were stored in baskets.

The three baskets (*tripitaka/tipitaka*) are:

● the basket of rules for monks and nuns (Vinaya Pitaka);

● the basket of discourses (Sutra/Sutta Pitaka);

● the basket of philosophical teaching (Abhidharma/Abhidhamma Pitaka).

The last of these collections is, on the whole, later than the other two and some portions of the Sutra and Vinaya Pitakas are considerably later than others.

**?** Draw a diagram which shows the three main parts of the Pali Canon.

Much of what we know about the life of the Buddha is taken from the Pali Canon. Many of the stories about his life which are familiar to Buddhists all over the world are from the later parts of this collection, for example the Jataka (a part of the Sutra Pitaka).

# Chapter 6 | *Siddhartha Gautama: His Birth and Early Life*

The Buddha of our own era was born in northern India some time around 500 BCE. His name was Siddhartha Gautama and his family were members of the Sakya clan.

---

## Many *Buddhas*

The word 'Buddha' means 'Awakened One'. There have been many *buddhas* in the past; there will be many more in the future.

According to Buddhist teaching, *buddhas* are beings who understand the world as it is. They are not confused about what things are really like. They are not buffeted about by powerful emotions such as anger and greed. They can remember all of their previous lives and they teach other beings how to escape from suffering.

**?**

1. Read the description of a *buddha* again. What do you think *buddhas* are?
   - gods;
   - supermen;
   - ordinary men;
   - extraordinary men.
   Give reasons for your answer.
2. Can any of these details about *buddhas* be classed as facts? If so, list them; if not, explain why.

---

Our information about Siddhartha (which means 'he whose aim will be accomplished') comes almost entirely from the Buddhist scriptures. As we saw in Chapter 5, however, these scriptures were not written for historical reasons. Although some scholars have tried to sift through the scriptures and find all the information about 'the historical Buddha', what we know about the Buddha as a person is probably more of a reflection of what the writers of the scriptures saw than a 'historically accurate' portrait.

There is no one simple 'Life of Buddha' story. There are many stories about the Buddha's life; it is not always easy to fit them together. A very simple guide is that the more elaborate and miraculous the story, the later the source.

The version of the Buddha's life story which is set out below is taken mainly from the Pali Canon.

**BIRTH EVENTS**  The earliest record of Siddhartha's birth is probably 'The Sutra of Wondrous and Marvellous Events'. This is one of the *sutras* (discourses) in the basket of discourses (Sutra Pitaka) of the Pali Canon.

Almost exactly the same story is told about the birth of an earlier *buddha* named Vipassin. One reason why these stories are so similar might be that the same kinds of events mark the birth of every *buddha*. This would fit quite well with the Buddhist teaching that all *buddhas* reveal the same truth whatever time and culture they are born into.

**?**  Can you think of any other reasons why the two stories might be so similar?

## The Buddha is Born

*The birth of the Buddha*

The stories about the births of Siddhartha and Vipassin tell of how the being who was destined for enlightenment (*bodhisattva/bodhisatta*) was born in a heavenly realm called the Tusita Heaven to prepare himself for his final birth.

From the Tusita Heaven, the *bodhisattva* entered the womb of his mother-to-be. Siddhartha's mother was Queen Maya, wife of King Suddhodana. Suddhodana was the leader of the Sakya clan. This is the reason why his son, Siddhartha, who became the Buddha, is often called 'the sage of the Sakyas' or Sakyamuni.

When the *bodhisattva* entered her womb, the queen dreamed that a white elephant (a sign of good fortune) had entered her side. Some nine months later, when she was on her way to stay with her parents, the queen gave birth to a baby boy whilst she was standing in a woodland glade, the Lumbini Grove.

The story tells us that the child was not born in the usual way but from his mother's side and that he was untouched by blood or birth fluids of any kind. As the child entered the world, the trees blossomed and two streams of water, one warm, one cool, flowed down from the sky. The baby took seven steps and announced that this was to be his last birth. Shortly after the birth of her child, Queen Maya died and was reborn in the Tusita Heaven.

**?**

1   What were the names of Siddhartha's mother and father?
2   What was the name of the heaven in which the *bodhisattva* was born before entering his mother's womb?
3   What does the word *bodhisattva* mean?
4   What does the title Sakyamuni mean and to whom is it applied?
5   What was the name of the other *buddha* whose birth followed the same pattern as Siddhartha's?
6   Why do you think the births of great people are sometimes linked with stories of unusual events?

## EARLY LIFE

We have very little information about Siddhartha's early life. The oldest accounts comment on just three episodes.

### The Visit of the Sage Asita

Shortly after the birth of Siddhartha, a venerable sage named Asita turned up at Suddhodana's palace and asked to see the child. When he looked at the baby, Asita was filled with joy and sadness at the same time. He was happy because he was able to see the child who would become a *buddha* and teach people how to put an end to suffering. He was sad because he knew that he would die before the child became a *buddha*.

*Asita's visit*

In some versions of the story Asita says that the young prince will become either a *buddha* or a world ruler.

**?**

Which of the two destinies do you think the prince's father would have preferred? Why?

## Siddhartha's Luxurious Lifestyle

The scriptures tell us that Siddhartha was carefully looked after, that he wore fine clothes and that he had three palaces – one for each of the Indian seasons. The same story is told about the Buddha Vipassin and also about a wealthy young man of noble background called Yasas who became one of the Buddha's disciples.

Some accounts add that Siddhartha also had a wife and a son. Other early accounts tell us that he renounced the world whilst still a 'black-haired lad in the prime of youth'. In other words, he left palace life before he was married.

**?**

1   Name the other two people whose lifestyle is described in the same way as that of Siddhartha.
2   Write down any reasons you can think of why these three people should all be described as having a comfortable lifestyle before renouncing the world.

## Siddhartha's Experience of Meditation

One day, whilst his father was ploughing a field (some accounts explain that it was a ceremonial ploughing before a festival), the young prince was sitting under a tree when he decided to try to meditate. Very quickly he deepened his meditation and reached a state of mental calm which had the qualities of detachment, rapture and bliss.

The main significance of this event lies in the fact that later in his life, when he had given up austerities and other forms of meditation, Siddhartha returned to the kind of meditation he practised as a boy. It was this kind of meditation which enabled him to obtain an understanding of things as they really are. That understanding made him a *buddha*.

## SIDDHARTHA RENOUNCES WORLDLY LIFE

The oldest account of the young prince deciding to give up worldly life and find an escape from suffering tells us that he thought about old age, sickness and death, three experiences no one can avoid.

In this account he decides to look for a solution to the dissatisfaction and pain caused by life's changes. He wants to find something which is not affected by birth, decay and death. So he abandons his life in the palace and becomes a wandering recluse.

The most famous and popular version of the renunciation is, however, that found in a much later text, the Jataka – a collection of stories about the Buddha's former lives. In the Jataka story, instead of just thinking about old age, sickness and death, the young prince (who in this account has been sheltered from all suffering by his father) actually meets an old man, a sick man and a corpse. He is deeply upset by

*The great renunciation*

them. Later, he sees a recluse who seems to have a kind of inner happiness. At this point Siddhartha decides to take up the life of a recluse himself.

**?**

1    How would you describe the differences between the two accounts?
2    Why do you think the Jataka version is more popular with Buddhists?
3    Write a letter from Siddhartha to his father explaining why it was the best thing for him to do; and a letter to Siddhartha from his father explaining why he has made a mistake.
4    What difference does it make to our understanding of the Buddha if (a) he was married; (b) he was not married?

## AUSTERITIES AND MEDITATION

Between his leaving home and his enlightenment, two events or periods stand out in the life of Siddhartha. These are his practice of severe austerities and his practice of meditation under two meditation teachers: Arada Kalama and Udraka Ramaputra.

### Siddhartha's Practice of Austerities

The young prince had already found that even the best kind of worldly life was unsatisfactory and so it was natural that he would want to try the opposite and practise austerities. Many of the recluses at the time of the Buddha did this.

The main idea behind the practice of austerities is that if a person keeps still for a while they soon start to experience sensations which are unpleasant. The body might become uncomfortable because it is being kept upright or because the ground on which it is lying is hard or bumpy. In addition, the person might experience feelings of hunger, thirst or loneliness.

Normally, all of these sensations and feelings make people want to do something to remove them, to get rid of the tension and discomfort they cause. But, as soon as we start trying to keep these unpleasant experiences away, we become involved in obtaining food and shelter, and this means jobs, responsibilities and all the involvements and unsatisfactoriness of worldly life.

Ascetics (people who practise austerities), however, try not to give in to the desire to get rid of any discomforts they might experience. They try to just accept the unpleasant sensations. They hope that eventually they will reach a point where they are no longer made uncomfortable by feelings of hunger, loneliness and so on. This is the state of equanimity, the state where pleasure and pain are treated alike.

Siddhartha practised austerities along with five other ascetics. He was the most determined and led the others in looking for ways of increasing his ability to deal with pain. He practised holding his breath until he experienced headaches which felt as though his head was being crushed with the point of a sword or being held over a fire of coals.

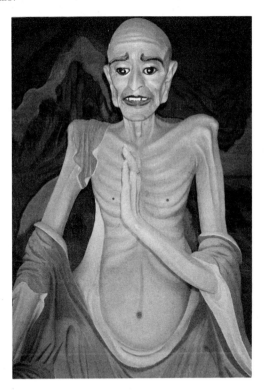

'. . . so did my ribs stick out through the little food.'

He fasted and became so thin and malnourished that he described himself in the following way:

> Then I thought, what if I now practise meditation without breathing. So I stopped breathing in and out from mouth and nose. And as I did so, there was a violent sound of winds issuing from my ears. Just as there is a violent sound from the blowing of a blacksmith's bellows, even so as I did so there was a violent sound. . . . And as I did so violent winds disturbed my head. Just as if a strong man were to crush one's head with the point of a sword, even so did violent winds disturb my head. . . .

[He practises holding his breath again three times, and the pains are as if a strap were being twisted round his head, as if a butcher were cutting his body with a sharp knife, and as if two strong men were holding a weaker one over a fire of coals.] Nevertheless such painful feeling as arose did not overpower my mind. . . .

Then I thought, what if I were to take food only in small amounts, as much as my hollowed palm would hold, juice of beans, vetches, chickpeas, or pulse. [He does so.] My body became extremely lean. . . . When I thought I would touch the skin of my stomach, I actually took hold of my spine, and when I thought I would touch my spine, I took hold of the skin of my stomach, so much did the skin of my stomach cling to my spine through the little food. When I thought I would ease myself, I thereupon fell prone through the little food. To relieve my body I stroked my limbs with my hand, and as I did so the decayed hairs fell from my body through the little food.

Some human beings seeing me then said, 'the ascetic Gotama [Gautama], is black.' Some said, 'not black is the ascetic Gotama, he is brown.' Others said 'not black is the ascetic Gotama nor brown, his skin is that of a mangura-fish,' so much had the pure clean colour of my skin been destroyed by the little food.

From the Mahasaccaka Sutta

Even after practising such austerities, Siddhartha still did not find an end to suffering. He realised that he would have to find another way.

1   What is the name for a person who practises austerity?
2   Explain in your own words what 'practising austerities' means.
3   Why did the Buddha decide to practise austerities?

## Siddhartha's Practice of Meditation

After renouncing worldly life, Siddhartha went to a meditation teacher named Arada Kalama and asked to become his disciple. Arada accepted him and taught the young prince all he knew. Siddhartha soon learnt all the practices Arada had shown him and became his teacher's equal. But he still did not find the way to escape from suffering. So, even though Arada offered to make Siddhartha the joint leader of his small group of recluses, the young man refused and went off to look for another teacher.

On leaving Arada, Siddhartha went to study under Udraka Ramaputra. Once again he learned everything Udraka had to teach. But he still did not find the way to escape from suffering. So, even though Udraka offered to make Siddhartha the leader of his whole group, the young man refused and went his own way.

1   What were the names of Siddhartha's two meditation teachers?
2   Explain the reasons why Siddhartha decided to leave Udraka in the form of a conversation between the two men. You might act this out in class.

**SIDDHARTHA BECOMES A BUDDHA**

In the Pali Canon we find a number of different accounts of the Buddha's enlightenment. One of them has Siddhartha leaving Udraka Ramaputra and settling outside a small town called Uruvela, 'a delightful spot with a pleasant grove, a river flowing delightfully with clear water and good fords, and round about a place for seeking alms'. After sitting down to meditate, he became enlightened.

Another account has Siddhartha practising austerities and coming to the conclusion that the way of the ascetic does not lead to the destruction of suffering. So he took food and drink and started to meditate in the same way that he had done when he was a boy. The five ascetics who were looking after him whilst he fasted were disgusted at Siddhartha's change of practice and abandoned him. They said '. . . the ascetic Gotama [Gautama] lives in abundance, he has given up striving and has turned to a life of abundance.' When they had left, Siddhartha deepened his meditation and became enlightened.

A third account has Siddhartha meditating on the bank of the Neranjara river. He is approached by Mara, the spirit of temptation, who encourages him to give up his quest, but Siddhartha resists. Then Mara send his armies against the young meditator. The armies are made up of lusts, aversions, cravings, hunger-and-thirst, cowardice, laziness, hypocrisy, stupidity and other such states of mind. In some accounts these feelings are said to be the daughters of Mara. Siddhartha resists all their temptations and goes on to become enlightened. In some versions of the story Mara says that Siddhartha is not worthy of enlightenment. In reply the prince touches the earth and calls on her to bear witness to the fact that he had worked his way towards Buddhahood over many lifetimes. The earth then testified to the truth of Siddhartha's claim by quaking.

*The temptation of Prince Siddhartha*

This event is a popular subject in Buddhist art. The meditating Buddha is often shown with his right hand over his right knee in the 'earth-touching gesture'.

**1**   What was the name of the town where, according to the first account, Siddhartha gained enlightenment?

**2**   Who was looking after Siddhartha in the second account?

**3**   By which river was Siddhartha sitting when he was tempted by Mara?

**4**   How might the story of the Buddha's temptation help you if you were a Buddhist?

## The Importance of the Enlightenment

One of the reasons why there are so many different accounts of the Buddha's enlightenment experience is that for some 200 years after his death everything anyone heard him say was passed on by word of mouth. Over such a long period of time the people who remembered what they had been told about the Buddha probably mixed up the order in which things happened.

Siddhartha probably did leave Udraka and go to meditate at Uruvela; he was probably abandoned by the five ascetics when he started to take food; he was probably tempted by a variety of worldly desires when he was meditating by the Neranjara river. What is unlikely is that he became enlightened in all these places.

For Buddhists, however, the place of his enlightenment is not the most important thing. What really matters is that he became enlightened, found the way which leads to the destruction of suffering and taught it to others.

Which matters most to a Buddhist?

**a** where the Buddha was enlightened;

**b** that the Buddha became enlightened;

**c** how the Buddha became enlightened.

Explain your choice.

But what is enlightenment? Turn back to pp. 34–6 (Chapter 4) and re-read the account of the Buddha's experience.

<table>
<tr><td>

| Chapter |
|:---:|
| **7** |

</td><td>

# *The Buddha's Teaching*

</td></tr>
</table>

Following his enlightenment, the Buddha sat and reflected on what he had experienced. These were the thoughts that passed through his mind:

> Mankind is intent on its attachments, and takes delight and pleasure in them . . . it is hard [for them] to see the principle of causality, origination by way of cause. Hard to see is the principle of the cessation of all compound things, the renunciation of clinging to rebirth, the extinction of all craving, absence of passion, cessation, *nirvana.*

**A GOD'S ADVICE**

After thinking along these lines the Buddha wondered whether there was any point in trying to tell people about what he had come to understand. Then one of the gods, Brahma Sahampati, appeared before the Buddha and pleaded with him. Brahma said, 'May the reverend Lord teach the Doctrine [about the nature of existence], may the well-gone one teach the Doctrine. There are beings of little impurity that are falling away through not hearing the Doctrine.'

After this vision the Buddha decided to share what he had discovered and to preach the Doctrine. But whom should he teach first? A spirit told him that the first two people who came to his mind – Arada Kalama and Udraka Ramaputra – were both dead. Then he thought of the five ascetics who had looked after him whilst he was practising austerities. With his Buddha-vision he learnt that they were staying in a deer park at Banares. So he set off for Banares.

**?**

1 What was the name of the god who asked the Buddha to share what he had discovered with others?

2 Why did the Buddha think most people would find difficulty in understanding his teaching?

3 Imagine that you were the Buddha. Why would you have decided to share your discovery with the five ascetics? Write your answer in the form of an address to them.

**THE BUDDHA'S FIRST SERMON**

When the Buddha arrived at the deer park in Banares, the five ascetics saw him in the distance and made a plan. They said, 'Here is Gotama who has taken up a life of abundance. We will not greet him, nor will we rise from our seats out of respect for him, nor will we take his bowl and robe as a sign of respect. We will let him sit down if he wants to though.'

However, when the Buddha came up to them one prepared a seat for him, one took his bowl and robe, whilst another set water down for him to wash his feet. Then the Buddha told them that he had awakened to the truth and found an end to suffering. After questioning him a little, three of the ascetics went looking for alms and the

Buddha shared his knowledge with the other two. When the three returned, the two went looking for alms and the Buddha taught the three. Soon afterwards all five became enlightened, they became *arhats/arahats* (worthy ones). These were the first members of the Buddhist community (*sangha*).

The next person to become enlightened was Yasas, the wealthy youth who had three palaces, one for each season (see p. 41). Soon 60 people had attained enlightenment and the Buddha sent them out to spread his teaching.

---

## Joining the *Sangha*

When a person decided to follow the Buddha they were admitted to the order of monks (the *sangha*) with a simple ceremony. First their heads were shaved, then they exchanged their ordinary clothes for orange robes and then they recited the Triple Refuge three times. This means that they took refuge in the Buddha, his Doctrine (*Dharma*) and his Community (*Sangha*). The three elements of Triple Refuge are also known as the Three Jewels or the Triple Gem.

---

1   Why do you think the five ascetics were not able to stick to their plan?
2   Who was the sixth disciple of the Buddha?
3   What is the title given to a follower of the Buddha who has become enlightened?

---

### 40 YEARS OF TEACHING AND PREACHING

The Buddha wandered around northern India teaching and preaching for about 40 years. Many of the events which occurred during that time have been preserved in the Buddhist scriptures. It would take many pages to relate them all. Two of the most famous, the founding of the order of nuns, and the dead child, are described below.

---

## The Founding of the Order of Nuns

Until the death of the Buddha's father, King Suddhodana, the community of those who had left household life in order to follow the Buddha was made up entirely of men. After the king died, however, the Buddha's stepmother, Mahaprajapati, requested that women be allowed to join the community. Three times she asked and three times the Buddha refused.

But Mahaprajapati was a very determined woman. She cut off her hair, put on orange robes and, along with some other women from the Sakya clan, followed the Buddha. When they arrived at the place where he was staying, they persuaded Ananda, the Buddha's personal attendant, to present their case. Three times Ananda asked the Buddha to admit women into the community and three times he refused. Then Ananda tried a different approach. He asked the Buddha whether a woman is capable of attaining enlightenment. The Buddha replied 'Yes'. Ananda followed this enquiry by reminding the Buddha that Mahaprajapati had been like a mother to him and fed him milk from her own breasts. At last the Buddha relented and said that he would allow women into the order if they would accept eight rules in addition to the 227 which regulated the lives of the monks. Mahaprajapti agreed to this and she and the other Sakyan women were ordained.

The eight additional rules for women are:

- a nun, no matter how senior, must always pay respects to a monk;

- a nun must spend the rainy season retreat (see pp. 56-7) in a place where there are monks;

- twice a month the nuns must ask the monks to give them teaching;

- the ceremony which ends the rainy season retreat must be performed by the nuns in front of the monks as well as before their own community;

- certain breaches of the rules must be dealt with by the assemblies of both monks and nuns and not by nuns alone;

- once a woman has trained to be a nun for two years she must ask both assemblies for admission into the community;

- a nun must never rebuke a monk;

- nuns may never offer official teaching to monks.

Later, when the Buddha was alone with Ananda, he announced that the true teaching would last for only 500 years because women had been admitted into the community. Had they not been admitted, it would have lasted for 1000 years.

### Is the founding of the order of nuns story true?

Some scholars have argued that this story does not go back to real events, but is a later invention by the monks. There are a number of reasons for this:

- the attitude shown by the Buddha towards women in this story is not the same as it is elsewhere in the scriptures;

- this event is stated to have taken place five years after the Buddha's enlightenment, but Ananda did not become the Buddha's attendant until 20 years after the enlightenment;

- this story makes Mahaprajapati the first nun, which conflicts with another account where a woman called Kisa Gotami is the first nun.

1    What was the name of the Buddha's stepmother?
2    What was the name of the Buddha's personal attendant?
3    How many times did the Buddha refuse to admit women into the order?
4    What do you think was the purpose of the eight additional rules for nuns? Discuss your views.
5    What reasons can you think of for the story that the Buddha originally refused to ordain women? Think of as many as you can.

## The Dead Child

In the city of Sravasti/Savatthi lived a woman named Kisa Gotami. Her son died soon after he had learned to walk. She became so upset and distraught that she put the child on her hip and went from house to house asking for medicine to bring him back to life. No one could help her. Then one man suggested that she went to the Buddha.

The Buddha, understanding her distress, did not say that he could or that he could not resurrect the child but praised her for having the sense to come to him. He told her to go to the city and bring back a mustard seed from a house where no one had died. Full of hope, she set off and went from house to house with her request. However, everywhere she went the story was the same: someone had died in that house. Eventually, she realised that the Buddha had set her a task to teach her a truth about life.

When she went back to the Buddha he asked her if she had obtained the seed. She told him that the purpose of the task had been achieved and requested to be admitted to the community (the *sangha*). Not long afterwards she attained enlightenment.

1   What was the name of the woman whose child died?
2   In which city did she live?
3   Why do you think the Buddha responded to her in the way he did?
4   What do you think is the central message of this story?
5   Would Kisa Gotami have been as likely to have got the message if the Buddha had simply told her that everyone dies? Give your reasons.

# Chapter 8

# *The Death of the Buddha*

The death of the
Buddha

The account of the Buddha's death that is preserved in the Pali Canon is one of the latest parts of that collection. It describes many miraculous events which occurred in the period just before he died. Some of the most well-known events are related below.

## THE BUDDHA'S DECISION TO DIE

Three months before his death the Buddha sat down with Ananda to eat the food they had collected from their alms-round near Vaisali/Vesali. The Buddha informed Ananda that those such as himself who had practised the four paths to power (the concentration of intention, the concentration of energy, the concentration of consciousness and the concentration of investigation) could remain alive for an aeon if they wished. He repeated this statement twice, but Ananda, being unreceptive to the hint, did not ask the Buddha to prolong his own life in this way.

When Ananda had left, Mara, the tempter, the lord of this world, approached the Buddha and tried to persuade him to leave the world. The Buddha's response was that he could not leave the world until his monks and nuns were learned and skilled enough to teach and explain his Doctrine. Mara pointed out that the monks and nuns could already do this. Then the Buddha said that he would not contemplate leaving the world until his teaching was flourishing, widely spread and well proclaimed by both gods and men. Again Mara pointed out that this had already happened.

At that point the Buddha told Mara that he would leave the world in three months' time. As soon as the Buddha agreed to give up his life, the earth quaked and the sky thundered. Later, when the Buddha told Ananda of his decision to pass away, Ananda realised that he had missed the chance of keeping the Buddha in the world.

1    Why do you think Mara wanted the Buddha to leave the world?
2    Why might Buddhists think it important that the Buddha's failure to stay in the world was Ananda's fault?
3    What does the dialogue between Mara and the Buddha tell Buddhists about the state of their religion?
4    Why could the Buddha choose when to die but we can't?

## THE BUDDHA'S EATING OF POISONED FOOD

The Buddha died of food poisoning. The story makes it clear, however, that this was not accidental. It explains how the Buddha, along with a group of disciples, went to Pava, near Kusinagara/Kusinara, and on the way stayed in the mango grove of Cunda (pronounced Chunda) the smith. Cunda had prepared three kinds of food for the Buddha's party: some hard, some soft and some *sukaramaddava*. Exactly what this last term means is not clear. Some writers think it refers to pork, others that it refers to mushrooms or truffles.

The Buddha told Cunda to serve his followers with the hard and soft food and himself with the *sukaramaddava* and then to dispose of the remaining *sukaramaddava* down a hole. Shortly after eating the meal the Buddha started to become sick. He did not, however, stay at the house of Cunda, perhaps fearing what might happen to the smith if his disciples decided that he had poisoned their teacher. Instead, he set off for Kusinagara with Ananda.

1    Where was the Buddha staying when he ate his last meal?
2    What was the food eaten by the Buddha at this meal?
3    What does this story tell us about the knowledge of a *buddha*?
4    How does this story link with the one about the Buddha's discussion with Mara concerning the time of his death?
5    Did Cunda poison the Buddha or did the Buddha poison himself or was it an accident? Give reasons for your answer.

## ANANDA'S DOUBT

On the way to Kusinagara the Buddha and Ananda came to a tree where the Buddha said he wanted to rest as he was in pain. Once seated the Buddha asked Ananda to fetch him a drink from a nearby stream. Ananda pointed out that the water would be undrinkable as 500 carts had just passed across the stream, but the Buddha insisted. Three times Ananda said it was useless to get water from the stream because it was all churned up; three times the Buddha asked him to go. Full of doubt, Ananda went to the stream with a bowl and lo! when he arrived the water was clear.

1 How many carts had just passed over the stream when the Buddha and Ananda arrived?

2 What does this story say about the relationship between the Buddha and nature?

After drinking the water and having a discussion with a passing traveller, the Buddha turned to Ananda and said,

> Ananda, it is possible that someone might provoke remorse in the goldsmith's son Cunda thus: 'It is no gain, it is loss for you, Cunda, that the Perfect One finally attained nibbana [*nirvana*] after getting his last alms food from you.' Now any such remorse of his must be countered thus: 'It is gain, it is great gain for you, Cunda, that the Perfect One finally attained nibbana after getting his last alms food from you. I heard and learned this from the Blessed One's own lips, friend Cunda: "These two kinds of alms food have equal fruit and equal ripening, and their fruit and ripening is far greater than any other's. What are the two? They are the alms food after eating which a Perfect One discovers the supreme full enlightenment and the alms food after eating which a Perfect One finally attains nibbana with the nibbana element without result of former clinging left. Cunda the goldsmith's son has stored up a deed that will lead to longevity, to good position, to happiness, to fame and to heaven." ' Any remorse of his must be countered thus.
>
> From the Mahaparinibbana Sutta

So not only was Cunda not to blame, he gained merit from providing the food.

Does this agree with your own answer to the question about who poisoned the Buddha?

## THE BUDDHA'S FUNERAL PYRE

Upon leaving the tree where he had rested, the Buddha, along with Ananda, journeyed on to the sala-tree grove belonging to the Mallian tribe just outside Kusinagara. Once there the Buddha told Ananda to go into Kusinagara and tell the Mallians that on that very night, in the last watch, the Buddha would attain final *nirvana*. Ananda passed on the message and in the first watch of the night the various Mallian families went to pay their respects to the Buddha.

The next morning, after the Buddha had died, Ananda and another monk went into Kusinagara and told the Mallians of the Lord's death. Despite being prepared for this news, many of the Mallians were overcome with grief for they knew that a *buddha* does not appear in the world very often.

Shortly afterwards, the Mallians began the funeral preparations for the Buddha's body. For seven days they paid honour to the Buddha with dancing and singing and by making garlands, perfumes and canopies out of cloth. At the end of the seven days they carried the Buddha's corpse to the east of Kusinagara and built a funeral pyre.

When they came to light the fire, however, it would not ignite. They asked the venerable Anuruddha about the reason for such a strange thing. Anuruddha told them that the reason the pyre would not light was that the venerable Maha Kasyapa and 500 monks were travelling towards Kusinagara to pay their respects to the Buddha. When Maha Kasyapa arrived at the site of the funeral pyre:

. . . he arranged his robe on one shoulder, and raising his hands palms together, he circumambulated the pyre three times to the right. Then the Blessed One's feet were revealed, and he saluted the Blessed One's feet with his head. And the five hundred Bhikkhus [monks] arranged their robes on one shoulder, and they did as the venerable Maha Kassapa had done. But as soon as they had finished, the pyre caught alight of itself. And just as when butter or oil burns it produces neither cinder nor ash, so too in the burning of the Blessed One's body neither the outer skin nor the inner skin nor the flesh nor the sinews nor the oil of the joints produced any cinder or ash: only the bones remained.

From the Mahaparinibbana Sutta

**?**

1   In what place did the Buddha die?
2   Who were the first people to be informed of the Buddha's death?
3   In what ways was the Buddha honoured for seven days after his death?
4   Why would the Buddha's funeral pyre not light?
5   How did the monks honour the Buddha after his death?
6   How many monks were travelling with Maha Kasyapa?
7   What do you think is the meaning of the story about the fire refusing to light and then igniting itself? Give reasons for your answer.

## THE BUDDHA'S REMAINS

After the cremation of the Buddha his bones were divided into eight parts and each part was given to a different tribe. The vessel in which the bones had been kept was given to the Brahmana Dona and the Buddha's ashes were given to the Moriyan tribe. Each of the people who had been given a part of the Buddha's remains built a monument over them. This is how the first pilgrimage sites of Buddhism came into existence.

*The great* stupa *at Sanchi – a later version of the mounds built over the Buddha's remains*

## HUMAN OR SUPERHUMAN?

The Buddha was 80 years old when he died. For 40 of those years he travelled around northern India teaching people what he had understood. During this time he acquired many followers and became quite famous. His life was filled with many interesting events, some of which have been related in this section. Although you can only get a detailed picture by reading all the accounts of his life, you should by now have acquired some idea of what the Buddha was like.

Some years ago, the presenter of a BBC film about Buddhism asked a well-known Sri Lankan Buddhist teacher whether the Buddha was a god, a human or a superhuman. The teacher's reply was that the Buddha was a man, an extraordinary man but definitely a man.

If we understand the Buddha as an extraordinary man, what does his life story tell us about the potential of human beings?

### Fact or Fiction?

If the evidence relating to the Buddha's life is examined it is clear that much of it is based on the experiences of a real person. The question is 'How much is fact and how much is fiction?' Many Buddhists think that it does not really matter because all the stories tell us something about the Buddha. What is seen by one disciple is not always seen by others. Is the 'truth' as seen by one person the 'whole truth' or just a part of it? Can we ignore any disciple's point of view if we are trying to understand how Buddhists think of the Buddha? The answer to the first question must be 'Just a part' and the answer to the second must be 'No'.

It may be that Siddhartha did not meet an old man, a sick man and a corpse, but it is clear from his teaching that old age, sickness and death were important issues for him. If you were trying to get someone to think about these subjects, which method do you think would be most successful – telling them that the Buddha gave these matters a lot of thought or telling them that he had disturbing encounters with an old man, a sick man and a corpse? On the whole, Buddhists tend to choose the second way, they use stories about people to pass on teachings which, in themselves, are quite abstract.

Do you think this is a good idea? Give reasons for your answer and discuss them as a class.

# Part III  THE DEVELOPMENT OF BUDDHISM

## Chapter 9

# *Monasteries*

During the time of the Buddha, his disciples began to give up the wandering life during the rainy season (July to October). Throughout that period of about three months the monks and nuns would gather together at settlements on the outskirts of towns and cities. Sometimes these settlements were made and maintained by the monks themselves. At other times they were paid for by wealthy lay followers. The huts in which the monks lived were called *viharas* and, as time went by, this word came to be used to refer to any Buddhist monastery.

*A Buddhist monastery in Tibet.*

This living together during the rainy season made the Buddhist *sangha* more united than the communities of other wandering recluses. In the years following the Buddha's death the custom of monks and nuns returning to the same *vihara* every rainy season became established. Eventually, wandering monks and nuns became quite unusual. Whilst this was often beneficial to the lay Buddhists who lived in the towns, and made life easier for the monks and nuns, it had at least one negative effect. The members of the various local *sanghas* met each other less and less. This eventually contributed to divisions occurring within the *sangha* as a whole.

**?**

1   What was the name given to the huts where the monks and nuns lived during the rainy season retreat?
2   What does this name refer to now?
3   What benefits might the lay Buddhists obtain from having a settled Buddhist community just outside their town?
4   Why do you think life was easier for the monks and nuns when they were living in the huts? List three reasons.

# Chapter 10

# *The Expansion of Buddhism in India*

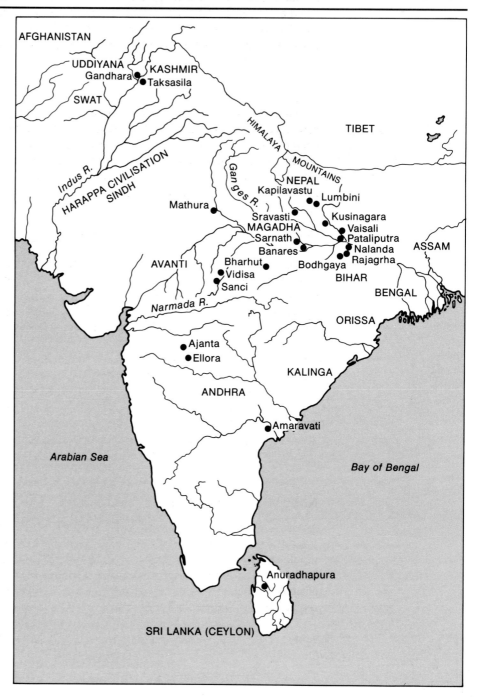

*Buddhist India*

Whilst the Buddha was alive, and for some time after his death, his teaching did not spread much beyond the basin of the River Ganges (see the map opposite). Then, during the reign of Asoka (269–232 BCE), Buddhism began to spread throughout India and beyond.

Asoka became emperor of India after a great battle in which many people were killed and maimed. Only one part of north-eastern India refused to submit to his rule. The battle changed Asoka's whole outlook. The waste of human life made him decide to give up conquest by fighting and, in future, to conquer by righteousness.

## THE GOLDEN AGE OF BUDDHISM IN INDIA

Asoka converted to Buddhism, though he did not require all his subjects to do the same. Rather, he encouraged all the different religious groups to have respect for each other and to be open to one another's teachings. He learned about Buddhist teachings from the monks of various schools and encouraged an atmosphere of religious tolerance. Evidence of this can be seen from the contents of his rock edicts, 14 inscriptions about the best way to lead one's life. These were carved on rock faces all over his empire.

He encouraged the lay people not to harm animals, to honour their parents, teachers and elders, and not to be over-greedy in the pursuit of wealth. Although the rock edicts present little that is specifically Buddhist – many other traditions held the same basic values – Asoka's own connection with Buddhism meant that the number of Buddhists grew at a rapid rate during his reign. Asoka also sent missionaries to South India, Burma, Sri Lanka, Afghanistan, Egypt and Greece. In many respects the time of Asoka represents the golden age of Buddhism in India.

1. What were the dates of Asoka's rule?
2. What made Asoka give up killing and decide to rule through righteousness?
3. Write out the basic principles set out in the rock edicts.
4. Imagine you are a Buddhist missionary sent out by Asoka. Write a letter to the head of your monastery telling him about your experiences.
5. If Asoka's principles were applied in our modern world what difference would it make to (a) your life and (b) international affairs?

## Not All Buddhists Were Committed

An unintended consequence of Asoka's support for Buddhism was that many of the people who became Buddhists, or who went further and were ordained as monks or nuns, lacked a true commitment to the religion. For many people, becoming a Buddhist offered personal benefits such as a more comfortable lifestyle or a better education. Not surprisingly, arguments broke out about the requirements for being a Buddhist and, in particular, for being a monk.

Why might state support for a religion sometimes lower the quality of religious life? Discuss your answers.

## BUDDHIST COUNCILS

Immediately after the Buddha's death, 499 *arhats*, along with Ananda, the Buddha's personal attendant, held a council at Rajagrha under the chairmanship of Maha Kasyapa. The purpose of this and all Buddhist councils was for the *sangha* to remind themselves of and agree upon the Buddha's teachings. About 100 years later a disagreement about proper behaviour for a monk led to a second council being convened at Vaisali. It appears that some kind of harmony and agreement resulted from this council. However, the underlying differences of opinion still remained. Consequently, within 50 years, another council was convened at Pataliputra. This time the disagreements could not be overcome and the *sangha* split into two groups.

### Divisions Within the *Sangha*

On one side were the Sthaviras (the Elders – predecessors of the modern Theravada school of Buddhism); on the other were the Mahasanghikas (the Great Community). Both groups claimed to have kept to the teaching of the Buddha. The Elders emphasised the importance of the monastic life, the authority of the monks and the humanity of the Buddha. Members of the Great Community, on the other hand, placed high value on lay as well as monastic life, they allowed lay disciples into their meetings and regarded the Buddha as superhuman.

Eventually, both of these schools subdivided even further, giving rise to the so-called 18 schools of early Buddhism.

**?**

1 Who chaired the first Buddhist council?
2 For what purpose are Buddhist councils held?
3 List the places at which the first three councils were held.
4 What were the names of the two groups which disagreed at the third council?
5 What were the main differences between them?
6 How do you think it feels to be part of a group which disagrees about and divides because of basic beliefs? Write down five 'feeling' words and then compare them with someone else's.

### Another Argument, Another Division

According to the texts of the Sthaviras, Asoka convened another council in the seventeenth year of his reign. This time it was to deal with a dispute within the school of the Elders. Asoka's council is usually referred to, rather misleadingly, as the third council. Although he might have been interested in the subtle differences in the teachings of the disputing parties, Asoka was probably more concerned to maintain a standard teaching for the guidance of his subjects.

The winning group later became the modern Theravada school. Asoka's own son Mahendra/Mahinda became a monk of this school, and he was the first Buddhist missionary to Sri Lanka. The losers, called the Sarvastivadins (those who teach that the past and the future are just as real as the present), had to give up teaching around the capital. They did, however, continue to attract a strong following in the north-west of India.

**1**  Why did Asoka take a keen interest in religious arguments?

**2**  Hold a discussion between (a) a Buddhist who says the teaching must be exactly right and (b) one who wants to put it in a form that most people can understand.

**3**  Why do some members of a society think it is important for everyone to agree on basic beliefs? Discuss your answers.

## BUDDHISM IN NORTH-WESTERN INDIA

The main route for the spread of Buddhism outside India was through the north-west of the country into Afghanistan and Central Asia. From there it travelled along the Silk Route into China. Since the time of Alexander the Great (known as Alexander the Barbarian to the Persians), the area to the north-west of India had been controlled by the descendants of the Greeks. They found Buddhist teachings quite attractive.

One Greek ruler who is well known to Buddhists was Menandros (Milinda in Pali). He ruled parts of northern India during the middle of the second century BCE. He is famous because a conversation between him and a Buddhisk monk, known as Dhitika by the Sarvastivadins and Nagasena by the Theravadins, has been preserved and now forms part of the Buddhist scriptures. As a result of this conversation, Menandros/Milinda is said to have converted to Buddhism and to have become a lay disciple. Here is a passage from that famous conversation:

### The Questions of King Milinda

In the land of the Bactrian Greeks there was a city called Sagala. Its king was Milinda, a man who was learned, experienced, intelligent and competent, and who at the proper times carefully observed all the appropriate Brahmanic rites. As a disputant he was hard to assail, hard to overcome, and he was recognised as a prominent sectarian teacher.

One day a numerous company of Arhats, who lived in a well-protected spot in the Himalayas, sent a messenger to the Venerable Nagasena, then at the Asoka Park in Patna, asking him to come, as they wished to see him. Nagasena immediately complied by vanishing from where he was and miraculously appearing before them. And the Arhats said to him: 'That king Milinda, Nagasena, constantly harasses the order of monks with questions and counter-questions, with arguments and counter-arguments. Please go, Nagasena, and subdue him!' But Nagasena replied: 'Never mind just this one king Milinda! If all the kings of India would come to me with their questions, I could well dispose of them, and they would give no more trouble after that! You may go to Sagala without any fear whatever!' And the Elders went to Sagala, lighting up the city with their yellow robes which shone like lamps, and bringing with them the fresh breeze of the holy mountains.

The Venerable Nagasena stayed at the Sankheyya hermitage together with 80 000 monks. King Milinda, accompanied by a retinue of 500 Greeks, went up to where he was, gave him a friendly and courteous greeting, and sat on one side. Nagasena returned his greetings, and his courtesy pleased the king's heart.

And King Milinda asked him: 'How is your Reverence known, and what is your name, Sir?' 'As Nagasena I am known, O great king, and as Nagasena do my fellow religious habitually address me. But although my parents give such names as Nagasena, or Surasena, or Virasena, or Sihasena, nevertheless this word "Nagasena" is just a conceptual term, a mere name. For no real person can here be apprehended.' But King Milinda explained: 'Now listen, you 500 Greeks and 80 000 monks, this Nagasena tells me that he is not a real person! How can I be expected to agree with that!' And to Nagasena he said: 'If, most reverend Nagasena, no person can be apprehended in reality, who then, I ask you, gives you what you require by way of robes, food, lodgings and medicines? Who is it that consumes them? Who is it that guards morality, practises meditation, and realises the [four] Paths and their Fruits, and thereafter Nirvana? For, if there were no person, there could be no merit and no demerit; no doer of meritorious or demeritorious deeds, and no agent behind them; no fruit of good and evil deeds, and no reward or punishment for them. If someone should kill you, O Venerable Nagasena, he would not commit any murder. And you yourself, Venerable Nagasena, would not be a real teacher, or instructor, or ordained monk! What then is this "Nagasena"? Are perhaps the hairs of the head "Nagasena"?' – 'No, great king!' 'Or perhaps the hairs of the body?' – 'No, great king!' 'Or perhaps the nails, teeth, skin, muscles, sinews, bones, marrow, kidneys, heart, liver, serous membranes, spleen, lungs, intestines, mesentery, stomach, excrement, the bile, phlegm, pus, blood, grease, fat, tears, sweat, spittle, snot, fluid of the joints, urine, or the brain in the skull – are they this "Nagasena"?' – 'No, great king!' – 'Or is form this "Nagasena", or feeling, or perceptions, or impulses, or consciousness?' – 'No, great king!' – Then is it the combination of form, feelings, perceptions, impulses, and consciousness?' – 'No, great king!' – 'Then is it outside the combination of form, feelings, perceptions, impulses, and consciousness?' – 'No, great king!' – 'Then, ask as I may, I can discover no Nagasena at all. Just a mere sound is this "Nagasena", but who is the real Nagasena? Your Reverence has told a lie, has spoken a falsehood! There really is no Nagasena!'

Thereupon the Venerable Nagasena said to King Milinda: 'As a king you have been brought up in great refinement and you avoid roughness of any kind. How then did you come – on foot, or on a mount?'

'I did not come, Sir, on foot, but on a chariot.' – 'If you have come on a chariot, then please explain to me what a chariot is. Is the pole the chariot?' – 'No, reverend Sir!' – 'Is then the axle the chariot?' – 'No, reverend Sir!' – 'Is it then the wheels, or the framework, or the flag-staff, or the yoke, or the reins, or the goad-stick?' – 'No, reverend Sir!' – 'Then is it the combination of pole, axle, wheels, framework, flag-staff, yoke, reins, and goad which is the "chariot"?' – 'No, reverend Sir!' – 'Then is this "chariot" outside the combination of pole, axle, wheels, framework, flag-staff, yoke, reins, and goad?' – 'No, reverend Sir!' – 'Then, ask as I may, I can discover no chariot at all. Just a mere sound is this "chariot". But what is the real chariot? Your Majesty has told a lie, has spoken a falsehood! There really is no chariot! Your Majesty is the greatest king in the whole of India. Of whom then are you afraid, that you do not speak the truth?' And he exclaimed: 'Now listen, you 500 Greeks and 80 000 monks, this king Milinda tells me that he has come on a chariot. But when asked to explain to me what a chariot is, he cannot establish its existence. How can one possibly approve of that?'

The 500 Greeks thereupon applauded the Venerable Nagasena and said to King Milinda: 'Now let your Majesty get out of that if you can!'

But King Milinda said to Nagasena: 'I have not, Nagasena, spoken a falsehood. For it is in dependence on the pole, the axle, the wheels, the framework, the flag-staff, etc., that there takes place this denomination "chariot", this conceptual term, a mere name.' – 'Your Majesty has spoken well about the chariot. It is just so with me. In dependence on the 32 parts of the body and the five Skandhas there takes place this denomination "Nagasena", this designation, this conceptual term, a current appellation and a mere name. In ultimate reality, however, this person cannot be apprehended. And this has been said by our Sister Vajira when she was face to face with the Lord:

> "Where all constituent parts are present,
> The word 'a chariot' is applied.
> So likewise where the skandhas are,
> The term a 'being' commonly is used." '

'It is wonderful, Nagasena, it is astonishing, Nagasena! Most brilliantly have these questions been answered! Were the Buddha himself here, he would approve what you have said. Well spoken, Nagasena, well spoken!'

*From the Milindapanha*

1    Compare this account with the teaching about no-self on p. 9.
2    Now write your own conversation on no-self between a Buddhist monk and a British teenager.

## Buddhist Art in North-Western India

The Greek artists of north-western India developed an artistic style known as Gandhara. Some of the most gracious and beautiful Buddhist images were made in this style (see photograph).

Head of the Buddha
*carved in the
Gandharan style*

# Chapter 11

# *The Rise of Mahayana Buddhism*

During this important phase of Buddhist expansion a new form of Buddhism was emerging. It drew followers from all of the Buddhist schools and called itself Mahayana (the Great Vehicle). Whilst the Sarvastivadins came to dominate the northern silk route from Kashgar through Aksu, Kucha and Karashahr, it was the Mahayanists who had the greatest influence along the southern silk route through Khotan, Niya and Miran (see the map on p. 96).

**?**

1 What was the name of the new Buddhist movement?
2 In which modern country are these ancient cities now located?
3 Try to find out the main religion of the people who live in this area now.

## THE MAHAYANA

The important thing to recognise about the Mahayana is that it was not a school in the same way that the Sthaviravada and the Sarvastivada were. Although these two schools disagreed about certain aspects of Buddhist teaching, what made them into separate schools was that they had different sets of rules (*vinaya*). Consequently the two sets of monks and nuns could not meet together for communal recitations of the rules. Mahayanists came from most, if not all, of the 18 schools of early Buddhism. They did not have their own code of discipline (*vinaya*) and were not, therefore, a separate school in the Buddhist sense.

Many of the Mahayana teachings can be found in the Pali Canon and in the canons of other schools. However, the Mahayanists did not present their views as interpretations of these canons. Rather, they produced new scriptures. In some of these texts the Mahayana teachings are put into the mouth of the Buddha. In others, a follower of the Mahayana, monk or lay, is the principal teacher. Most of the Mahayana scriptures present those who accept the non-Mahayana view of Buddhism as inferior. All non-Mahayanists are grouped together as Hinayanists (followers of the inferior vehicle: *hina-yana*). The non-Mahayanists did not like to be called Hinayanists but they never came up with another word to refer to themselves. So, whenever the word Hinayana is used in this book its meaning is simply 'non-Mahayana'.

**?**

1 What is the main principle which separates one Buddhist school from another?
2 Why was the Mahayana not a new school?
3 By what name did the Mahayanists refer to other Buddhists?

## Mahayana Scriptures

One of the main differences between the Mahayanists and other Buddhists concerned the scriptures. The Mahayanists regarded their own scriptures, the Mahayana Sutras, as possessing the authority of the Buddha. The other Buddhists did not accept this. The Mahayana scriptures include stories which explain why they contain higher teachings than other Buddhist scriptures. One such story is found in the Lotus Sutra. It is called 'The Parable of the Burning House'.

### *The Parable of the Burning House*

Sariputra! Suppose in a [certain] kingdom, city, or town, there is a great elder. His house is spacious and large, but it has only one door, and many people dwell in it. Its halls and chambers are decayed and old, its walls crumbling down, the bases of its pillars rotten, the beams and roof-trees toppling and dangerous. On every side, at the same moment, fire suddenly starts. The boys of the elder are in the dwelling. The elder, on seeing this fire spring up on every side, is greatly startled and reflects thus: 'Though I am able to get safely out of the gate of this burning house, yet my boys in the burning house are pleasurably absorbed in amusements without knowledge or fear. Though the fire is pressing upon them and pain and suffering are instant, they do not mind or fear and have no impulse to escape.'

Sariputra! This elder ponders thus: 'This house has only one gate, which moreover is narrow and small. My children are young, knowing nothing as yet, and attached to their place of play; perchance they will fall into the fire and be burnt.'

Then the elder reflects thus: 'This house is burning. If I and my children do not get out at once, we shall certainly be burnt up by it. Let me now, by some means, cause my children to escape this disaster.' Knowing that to which each of his children will joyfully respond, the father calls them, saying: '[Here are] rare and precious things for your amusement – if you do not [come] and get them, you will be sorry for it afterwards. So many goat-carts, deer-carts, and bullock-carts are now outside the gate to play with. All of you come quickly out of this burning house, and I will give you whatever you want.' Thereupon the children, hearing of the attractive playthings mentioned by their father, and because they suit their wishes, every one eagerly, each pushing the other, and racing one against another, comes rushing out of the burning house.

Then the elder, seeing that his children have safely escaped and are all in the square, sits down in the open, no longer embarrassed, but with a mind at ease and ecstatic with joy. Then each of the children says to the father: 'Father! Please now give us those playthings you promised us – goat-carts, deer-carts, and bullock-carts.' Sariputra! Then the elder gives to his children equally each a great cart. . . . It is yoked with white bullocks of pure [white] skin, of handsome appearance, and of great muscular power . . . and also it has many servants and followers to guard them. Wherefore? Because this great elder is of boundless wealth and all his various storehouses are full to overflowing. So he reflects thus: 'My possessions being boundless, I must not give my children inferior small carts. . . . Meanwhile, each of the children rides on his great cart, having received that which he had never before had and never expected to have.'

Sariputra! What is your opinion? Has that elder, in [only] giving great carts . . . to his children equally, been in any way guilty of falsehood?

'No, World-honoured One!' says Sariputra. 'That elder only caused his children to escape the disaster of fire and preserved their bodies alive – he committed no falsity. Why? He thus preserved their bodies alive, and in addition gave them the playthings they obtained;

moreover, it was by his trick that he saved them from that burning house! World-honoured One! Even if that elder did not give them one of the smallest carts, still he is not false. Wherefore? Because that elder from the first formed this intention, "I will, by a trick, cause my children to escape." For this reason he is not false. How much less so seeing that, knowing his own boundless wealth and desiring to benefit his children, he gives them great carts equally!'

From the Lotus Sutra

The message of this story is that although different Buddhist groups disagree about what the Buddha actually taught it does not really matter. All these teachings were simply designed for people with different abilities. In the end all will reach the same goal, just as all the children received the same cart.

The ability to adapt his teachings to the needs of the audience is called the Buddha's skill-in-means (*upaya kausalya*). The Mahayanists used this skill-in-means to adapt their teachings to local conditions. Such flexibility was especially useful when presenting Buddhism to non-Indian people who might not be familiar with ideas about rebirth or who did not have monks and nuns in their country.

**?**

1   At the end of the parable of the burning house, the Buddha asks Sariputra whether the father had lied to the children. Sariputra says, 'No, it might have seemed like a lie but it was really just skilful behaviour.' What do you think? Justify your reasons.

2   What did the Mahayanists call the ability to change the teachings of the Buddha according to the needs of the audience?

## MAHAYANA AND HINAYANA

The difference between a Mahayana teaching and a Hinayana one on the same subject was often just a matter of emphasis. On some points though, the disagreement is quite pronounced. For example, most Hinayana schools accepted three types of enlightened beings. First were the *buddhas*, who discovered the truth for themselves and then taught it to anyone who was interested. Second were the *pratyeka buddhas*, those who discovered the truth for themselves but who did not teach in the same way. Third were the *arhats*, those who had discovered the truth by listening to a *buddha*, meditating on what they had been taught and then putting what they had learned into practice. Many Mahayanists had doubts about the enlightenment of some *arhats*.

### The *Arhats*

After the Buddha's death, the *arhats*, the worthy ones, were the most senior Buddhist teachers. These early *arhats* all claimed to have reached the three knowledges that the Buddha himself obtained on the night of his enlightenment (see pp. 34–6). At the time when the Mahayana was developing, a new kind of *arhat* was becoming known. These *arhats* were called the dry-visioned ones. They claimed to have attained the third of the Buddha's knowledges: destruction of the *asravas* (i.e. the three limitations on understanding described on pp. 35–6) and would not therefore be born again; but they also claimed not to be able to remember the past lives of themselves and others. For many Mahayanists the claims of these dry-visioned *arhats* seemed highly suspicious.

## Higher Level Teaching

At about the same time that the new *arhats* were coming on the scene, some Buddhists were having visionary experiences in which the Buddha appeared to them and gave them a higher level teaching. It was this teaching that came to form the core of the Mahayana scriptures. Because the Buddha appeared to disciples in visions, the Mahayanists were not able to agree with Hinayana schools about the humanity of the Buddha. Mahayanists regarded the Buddha not only as superhuman but also as possessing a level of wisdom and compassion way beyond that of the *arhats*. For the Mahayanists, becoming an *arhat* was not the final goal for a Buddhist. In their view a Buddhist should try to become a *buddha*. Only as a *buddha* was it possible to help all beings. As far as the Mahayanists were concerned, a person who was aiming to become a *buddha* was superior to an *arhat*. They called these *buddhas*-to-be 'bodhisattvas' (awakening beings).

## *Bodhisattvas*

The early Buddhists and the Hinayanists also used the word *bodhisattva*. In their scriptures, however, *bodhisattva* always means the being who was to become the Buddha Sakyamuni. The Mahayanists simply extended this idea of a *buddha*-to-be to include all people who were aiming for Buddhahood. Some of the later Mahayana writings divided the *bodhisattva*'s progress into stages, starting with the moment he or she makes a vow to become a *buddha* for the benefit of all beings and ending with the moment of awakening (*bodhi*). In some texts these stages are linked with the *bodhisattva*'s practice of the spiritual perfections (*paramita*).

---

### *The six perfections*

Developing the perfections was a practice already common in the Sarvastivada school and the Mahayanists probably borrowed it from them. Although the eightfold path is the most well-known system of Buddhist training, even the earliest Buddhist scriptures contain accounts of other ways to the same goal. The 'seven limbs of enlightenment' is one example of such a scheme; the cultivation of the perfections is another. In the earliest Mahayana accounts, there are six perfections:

1 giving (*dana*);
2 morality (*sila*);
3 patience (*ksanti*);

4 energy (*virya*);
5 concentration (*samadhi*);
6 insight or wisdom (*prajna*).

---

Here is a story about the Buddha when he was still a *bodhisattva*. It illustrates the perfection of giving.

## The Hungry Tigress

The Buddha told the following story to Ananda: 'Once upon a time, in the remote past, there lived a king, Maharatha by name. He was rich in gold, grain, and chariots, and his power, strength and courage were irresistible. He had three sons who were like young gods to look at. They were named Mahapranada, Mahadeva, and Mahasattva.

'One day the king went for relaxation into a park. The princes, delighted with the beauties of the park and the flowers which could be seen everywhere, walked about here and there until they came to a large thicket of bamboos. There they dismissed their servants, in order to rest for a while. But Mahapranada said to his two brothers: "I feel rather afraid here. There might easily be some wild beasts about, and they might do us harm." Mahadeva replied: "I also feel ill at ease. Though it is not my body I fear for. It is the thought of separation from those I love which terrifies me." Finally, Mahasattva said:

> "No fear feel I, nor any sorrow either,
> In this wide, lonesome wood, so dear to Sages.
> My heart is filled with bursting joy,
> For soon I'll win the highest boon."

'As the princes strolled about in the solitary thicket they saw a tigress, surrounded by five cubs, seven days old. Hunger and thirst had exhausted the tigress, and her body was quite weak. On seeing her, Mahapranada called out: "The poor animal suffers from having given birth to the five cubs only a week ago! If she finds nothing to eat, she will either eat her own young, or die from hunger!" Mahasattva replied: "How can this poor exhausted creature find food?" Mahapranada said: "Tigers live on fresh meat and warm blood." Mahadeva said: "She is quite exhausted, overcome by hunger and thirst, scarcely alive and very weak. In this state she cannot possibly catch any prey. And who would sacrifice himself to preserve her life?" Mahapranada said: "Yes, self-sacrifice is so difficult!" Mahasattva replied: "It is difficult for people like us, who are so fond of our lives and bodies, and who have so little intelligence. It is not at all difficult, however, for others, who are true men, intent on benefiting their fellow-creatures, and who long to sacrifice themselves. Holy men are born of pity and compassion. Whatever the bodies they may get, in heaven or on earth, a hundred times will they undo them, joyful in their hearts, so that the lives of others may be saved."

'Greatly agitated, the three brothers carefully watched the tigress for some time, and then went towards her. But Mahasattva thought to himself: "Now the time has come for me to sacrifice myself! For a long time I have served this putrid body and given it beds and clothes, food and drink, and conveyances of all kinds. Yet it is doomed to perish and fall down, and in the end it will break up and be destroyed. How much better to leave this ungrateful body of one's own accord in good time! It cannot subsist for ever, because it is like urine which must come out. Today I will use it for a sublime deed. Then it will act for me as a boat which helps me to cross the ocean of birth and death. When I have renounced this futile body, a mere ulcer, tied to countless becomings, burdened with urine and excrement, unsubstantial like foam, full of hundreds of parasites – then I shall win the perfectly pure Dharma-body, endowed with hundreds of virtues, full of such qualities as trance and wisdom, immaculate, free from all substrata, changeless and without sorrow." So, his heart filled with boundless compassion, Mahasattva asked his brothers to leave him alone for a while, went to the lair of the tigress, hung his cloak on a bamboo, and made the following vow:

> "For the weal of the world I wish to win enlightenment, incomparably wonderful. From deep compassion I now give away my body, so hard to quit, unshaken in my mind. That enlightenment I shall now gain, in which nothing hurts and nothing harms, and which the Jina's sons have praised. Thus shall I cross to the Beyond of the fearful ocean of becoming which fills the triple world!"

'The friendly prince then threw himself down in front of the tigress. But she did nothing to him. The Bodhisattva noticed that she was too weak to move. As a merciful man he had taken no sword with him. He therefore cut his throat with a sharp piece of bamboo, and fell down near the tigress. She noticed the Bodhisattva's body all covered with blood, and in no time ate up all the flesh and blood, leaving only the bones.

'It was I, Ananda, who at that time and on that occasion was that prince Mahasattva.'

From the Lotus Sutra

1 To whom did the term *bodhisattva* originally refer?
2 What are the six perfections (*paramita*)?
3 Choose one of the six perfections and write a story about a *bodhisattva* who is trying to cultivate it. Pay particular attention to the difference between the ordinary understanding of that quality and the perfection of it.

## Heavenly *Bodhisattvas*

Whilst most *bodhisattvas* would be reborn in an earthly situation, some of the most advanced ones were believed to have been reborn in heavenly realms. In the Buddhist view of the universe the heavens are places where life is much happier than on earth. Also, the beings who live in the heavens can see us even though we cannot see them. The heavens are not, however, outside *samsara*. They are constantly changing, and although beings must have built up a great deal of merit to be reborn there, eventually, after a long life of thousands of years, they will die and be reborn somewhere else.

### *Helping beings on earth*

Beings are born in the heavenly worlds because of their good deeds. From these worlds they can also help those beings who live on earth. This is one reason why advanced *bodhisattvas* choose to live in the heavens – from there they can help more people than if they lived on earth. Such help often comes in the form of teachings. A heavenly *bodhisattva* can appear to an earthly person in a vision or in the form of another earthly being. For example, the *bodhisattva* Maitreya (the next Buddha) is said to have appeared to a Mahayanist monk called Asanga and taught him about the way in which the mind confuses people and keeps them trapped in *samsara*. When Asanga put these teachings into a form that other people could understand he founded the Yogacara school. Yogacara is one of the two schools of philosophy in Mahayana Buddhism. It means 'yoga practice'. Its main concern is with the practice of meditation but, at the same time, it seeks to offer a description of human experience. This is what makes it a philosophy.

1 What qualities do the heavenly and earthly realms have in common?
2 How does a being get to be born in a heavenly world?
3 Which *bodhisattva* gave the Yogacara teachings to Asanga?
4 What is the main way that heavenly *bodhisattvas* help earthly beings?
5 What do you think is the purpose of the stories about heavenly *bodhisattvas*? What value have they for Buddhists?

## SOME FAMOUS BODHISATTVAS

Compassion (*karuna*) is one of the two principal qualities that all Mahayana Buddhists try to develop. The other is wisdom or insight (*prajna*). In the heavenly realms are two *bodhisattvas* who represent perfect compassion and perfect wisdom. They are called Avalokitesvara and Manjusri.

### *Wisdom*

Wisdom is understanding that nothing in this world exists in its own right. Everything and everybody is part of the great universal process. All things only exist because of other things and everything is interconnected (see pp. 24–5). For

Buddhists, seeing this is to understand the way things really are. From the Mahayana point of view, however, wisdom is not enough. The *arhats* who escaped rebirth through understanding lacked compassion for the sufferings of others.

## Compassion

Compassion is a concern for the welfare of others, a willingness to help others and a sensitivity to the pain and unhappiness of others. Think of a man who dreams he is drowning. He suffers and struggles and experiences fear. A person who understands what is really happening knows that the man is not really drowning and that his pain is not real. To know the truth is to have wisdom. However, wisdom without compassion can be cold. The wise man who does not have compassion might leave the dreamer to awaken on his own. The person with both wisdom and compassion will try to awaken the dreamer in a gentle manner.

## Bodhisattvas *seek both wisdom and compassion*

*Bodhisattvas* aim to develop both wisdom and compassion so that they can help beings in the best possible way. The need for compassion is clear, but how necessary is wisdom? Is compassion alone not enough? The Buddhist answer is definitely 'No'. Compassion without wisdom is blind. Compassion is easily misdirected. Everyone knows the kind of havoc that foolish do-gooders can create. The representatives of aid agencies such as Oxfam and Action Aid have many stories to tell about the damage caused by compassionate people trying to help others in inappropriate ways.

**?**

1  Name the *bodhisattvas* who represent perfect compassion and perfect wisdom.
2  Fill in the following blanks:
   *karuna* means _____;
   *prajna* means _____.
3  Write out Buddhist views on the following statements:
   ● wisdom without compassion is cold;
   ● compassion without wisdom is blind.
   Try to find examples which illustrate these views.

## Avalokitesvara

Avalokitesvara is the *bodhisattva* who represents perfect compassion. His concern is not simply to lead beings towards enlightenment, he also tries to help them deal with the problems of everyday life. Many Mahayana Buddhists pray to Avalokitesvara for help with all kinds of things.

There are a number of stories and paintings about the ways in which Avalokitesvara helps people. Because of his magical powers he can appear in any form he chooses. For example, he can appear as a *buddha*, as an old beggar, as a woman, as a saint of another religion or as a god. The numerous heads and arms on the picture (p. 71) show us that Avalokitesvara looks down to see how he can help beings and that he has many ways of offering help.

The Dalai Lama, leader of the Tibetan Buddhists (see Chapter 18), is thought by his followers to be an incarnation of Avalokitesvara. It is easy to understand why. His efforts to get the Chinese invaders to leave Tibet and make his country

*Avalokitesvara, the lord who looks down. The Tibetans call him Chen Rezi; the Chinese think of Avalokitesvara as a female and call her Kuan Yin.*

independent again won him the Nobel Prize for Peace in 1989. The Dalai Lama has never recommended violence as a way of freeing Tibet. He has always looked for a peaceful solution which would cause the minimum of suffering. Many people would say that this attitude shows not only his great compassion but also his deep wisdom.

## Manjusri

Wisdom or insight can, perhaps, be regarded as the essence of Buddhist teaching. In Mahayana Buddhism, wisdom is the last of the six perfections. To attain the perfection of wisdom is to attain enlightenment.

Look at the picture of Manjusri on p. 72. The sword in his right hand represents the insight which cuts away the veil of ignorance from the mind. In his left hand he holds a book. This is one of the Mahayana scriptures called 'The Perfection of Wisdom'. Manjusri rides on a lion, perhaps because the name given to the preaching of the Doctrine (*Dharma*) by a *buddha* or *bodhisattva* is a 'lion's roar'.

**?**

1 What is the Chinese name for Avalokitesvara?
2 What is the Tibetan name for Avalokitesvara?
3 Name the Tibetan leader who is thought to be an incarnation of Avalokitesvara.
4 Find out more about the Nobel Prize for Peace and people who have received it. What other Nobel prizes are there?

*Manjusri, the one of gentle glory*

**5**    Try to find out more about the Dalai Lama. This would be a good subject for a project but remember to concentrate on his religious significance.

**6**    Name the book on Manjusri's left.

## Maitreya

One difference between Mahayana and non-Mahayana Buddhists is their views about heavenly *bodhisattvas*. Mahayanists teach that there are many heavenly *bodhisattvas* who help beings in a number of ways. The non-Mahayanists accept only one heavenly *bodhisattva*: Maitreya.

The non-Mahayanists say that Maitreya is currently living in the Tusita Heaven, where Sakyamuni Buddha lived before taking his final birth (see Chapter 6).

Maitreya will be the next Buddha. Theravada Buddhists often try to make merit in the hope that, in the future, they will be reborn when Maitreya (Metteya in Pali) preaches the *Dharma* and that they will be able to attain enlightenment under his guidance.

Maitreya is also important in Mahayana Buddhism. He is believed to appear to people on earth in order to teach them (see, for example, the story of Asanga, on p. 69).

The image of Maitreya changes tremendously in different countries. Each of the pictures on the next page is a representation of Maitreya.

*Mi-lo-Fo (Chinese)*

*Maitreya (Sanskrit)*

*Miroku (Japanese)*

**?**  Look at these pictures. Which seems most different from the others?

The Mi-lo-Fo image is the most different. Chinese Buddhists regarded the monk whose image this is as Maitreya come to earth. His big belly and his bag of wonderful things represent wealth. His relaxed manner indicates spiritual contentment and the children show that he is happy with big families and lots of children. For the Chinese, all these are good signs and suitable characteristics for someone who is going to bring happiness into the world.

**?**

1   Link the different spellings of Maitreya with the appropriate language:

Maitreya     Japanese
Metteya      Chinese
Mi-lo-Fo     Sanskrit
Miroku       Pali

2   Name the heaven where Maitreya lives at present.

3   Write three sentences about the Buddhist belief in future *buddhas*. You might get some ideas from looking at the pictures of Maitreya.

## THE PURE LAND

One collection of Mahayana scriptures, called the Pure Land Sutras, introduced a teaching which later became very important in Chinese and Japanese Buddhism. This was the teaching about the Pure Land. In these texts we are introduced to the story of the *bodhisattva* Dharmakara (treasury of *dharma*). The story tells how, millions of years ago, Dharmakara listened to the preaching of a *buddha* from that time. He was so impressed that he decided to become a *buddha* himself.

*Amitabha*

However, Dharmakara did not want to preach the *Dharma* in a universe where it was very difficult for beings to make spiritual progress. So he meditated and performed good deeds for many lifetimes. Then he used all the merit he had accumulated to create a pure land where all the beings who lived there would find it easy to meditate and achieve *nirvana*. When he became a *buddha* he preached the *Dharma* in that pure land and came to be known as Amitabha, the Buddha of infinite light. The Chinese and Japanese names for Amitabha are A-mi-t'o (Chinese) and Amida (Japanese).

### Amitabha's Power

The Pure Land Sutras tell us that beings will benefit in many ways just from hearing Amitabha's name. For example, *bodhisattvas* who hear his name will never fall away from the three jewels of *Buddha*, *Dharma* and *Sangha* (see p. 48) – in other words, they will always be Buddhist. Women who hear his name will never have the misfortune to be born as females again.

The *sutras* state that those who have started out on the path to enlightenment and who meditate on Amitabha with faith will, when they die, be met by Amitabha and his disciples and be guided to the Pure Land. Even wrongdoers can be reborn in the Pure Land if they repent their bad deeds and improve their behaviour.

1  What was the name of the *bodhisattva* who became the Buddha Amitabha?
2  What do the benefits of hearing Amitabha's name tell us about early Buddhist attitudes to women?

## THE BODIES OF THE BUDDHA

From the time of the Buddha onwards his followers understood that he was more than just the person called Siddhartha. They said that the Buddha 'embodied' his teachings. This means that the way he looked, spoke and acted all displayed what he taught. He was a living example of the *Dharma* he preached. So the early Buddhists said that he had two bodies: a form body (*rupa kaya*) which was his physical being; and a truth body (*dharma kaya*) which was his teaching.

When speaking to a man named Vakkali the Buddha said,

> Whoso sees Dhamma [*Dharma*] sees me; whoso sees me sees Dhamma.
> Seeing Dhamma, Vakkali, he sees me; seeing me, he sees Dhamma.

The Mahayanists added another body to these two. They called it the enjoyment body (*sambhoga kaya*). The enjoyment body is the body seen by *bodhisattvas* when they have a vision of the Buddha. The form taken by the Buddha Amitabha in his Pure Land is his enjoyment body. Enjoyment bodies are fantastic to look at. Light shines from their every pore. The words spoken by the enjoyment body are sweet to hear and awaken the mind. Its fragrance is delightful. Buddhists say that the experience of the Buddha's enjoyment body is a spiritually uplifting one. Some later Mahayana texts state that it was through his enjoyment body that the Buddha preached the Mahayana scriptures.

Enjoyment bodies can create as many form bodies as they wish in order to help living beings. These form bodies are creations of the Buddha's skill-in-means (see p. 66), just as the enjoyment bodies themselves are creations of the Buddha's truth body as a skilful way of revealing the truth. In fact, the whole of Buddhism can be seen as the skilful activity of the truth body, which continually works for the awakening of all living beings.

## A Summary

The truth body of the Buddha is the entire universe as it is in itself (rather than as it is experienced by ignorant beings). In order to show beings the way things really are, the truth body creates enjoyment bodies. These are what would be called gods or heavenly beings in some religions. Enjoyment bodies create form bodies for particular purposes, such as the one the Buddha took for preaching the *Dharma* in northern India in the fifth century BCE.

?

1   Link the English word with its Sanskrit equivalent:
truth body            *rupa kaya*
enjoyment body        *dharma kaya*
form body             *sambhoga kaya*

2   In which body did the Buddha preach the Mahayana scriptures?

3   **a** Collect as many pictures of the Buddha as you can. Try to discover what the message (or messages) behind each picture is/are.

   **b** Decide which one you prefer. Explain your choice to someone else or in a class discussion.

## NAGARJUNA AND THE TEACHING OF EMPTINESS

*Nagarjuna*

Most followers of Mahayana Buddhism regard a man named Nagarjuna as one of their greatest teachers. He founded the Mahayana philosophical school called the Madhyamaka (the Middle Position school). Nagarjuna criticised many of the non-Mahayana Buddhists because he said that they had misunderstood the Buddha's teaching. They claimed that the elements which make up the world do not depend on anything else for their existence, they are 'self-existent'. This, of course, goes against the Buddha's teaching on dependent origination (*pratitya samutpada*) – see Chapter 4).

Nagarjuna said that nothing was self-existent, everything was dependently originated or empty of self-existence. He called this teaching the teaching of emptiness (*sunyata*). For Nagarjuna, as for the Buddha, the only things that exist are those which come into existence because of other things, in dependence on other things.

Many people have misunderstood Nagarjuna's teaching. Because Nagarjuna used the words empty (*sunya*) and emptiness (*sunyata*) they thought that he meant nothing exists. In fact, he was simply saying that none of the things which do exist does so in its own right, all things depend on other things, they are all interconnected.

**?**

1   What does *madhyamaka* mean?
2   Who was the founder of the Madhyamaka school?
3   In what way did Nagarjuna think some Buddhists had misunderstood the Buddha's teaching?
4   Explain Nagarjuna's teaching in your own words.

<table>
<tr><td>

**Chapter**

**12**

</td><td>

# *Tantra and Mantra –*
# *The Third Major Vehicle*

</td></tr>
</table>

In the early Buddhist scriptures the Buddha's first teaching of the four noble truths is often called 'the turning of the wheel of *dharma*' or 'the setting in motion of the wheel of *dharma*'. The idea behind this title is that with this teaching the Buddha established what we now call Buddhism. The early Mahayana Sutras are sometimes said to represent the second turning of the wheel of *dharma*, since they present Buddhist teaching in a way which is quite different from that found in the earlier literature.

Some time around the sixth century CE a third turning of the wheel of *dharma* was proclaimed. The followers of this new way called it Mantrayana (the Vehicle of Chants) or Vajrayana (the Diamond Vehicle) or Tantrayana (the Vehicle of Patterns). They distinguished themselves from the followers of the other two vehicles or traditions of Buddhism much as the Mahayanists had distinguished themselves from the non-Mahayanists.

**?**

1 What does the phrase 'turning the wheel of *dharma*' mean?
2 Name the three turnings of the wheel of *dharma*.

Three characteristics of the Tantrayana stand out as being distinctive. First is the emphasis placed on the individual teacher (*guru*). Second is the use of magical sounds (*dharani*) and chants (*mantra*). Third is the importance given to ritual.

### THE GURU

At the heart of all forms of Buddhism are the three jewels of the Buddha, the *Dharma* and the *Sangha*. Many Tantric Buddhists added a fourth, the teacher (*Guru*). The teacher was a person who was either enlightened or close to enlightenment, and was expert in skilful means. One of the skills needed by a teacher was the ability to understand the mind of his student(s) so that he could recommend the kind of practice that would enable them to attain enlightenment in the shortest possible time. Whereas the Mahayana scriptures had made the journey to enlightenment take many lifetimes, the Tantric teachers tried to help their students attain it during their present life.

Many of the Indian Tantric teachers were called perfected ones (*siddha*). Later it became important for followers of Tantric Buddhism to prove that they had received their teaching from a true Buddhist master. So, for example, Buddhists of the Tibetan Kagyu school (see pp. 116–17) trace their teachers back through the saint Milarepa and his teacher Marpa to the Indian *siddhas* Naropa and Tilopa.

According to Tantric Buddhist teaching, not until a student has been initiated by a proper teacher will he or she be able to practise the Tantric rituals successfully. Sometimes initiation ceremonies are called 'empowerments' because the teacher uses some of his own spiritual power to begin the process of awakening in the student's mind. In some texts we are told that a teacher can completely awaken a student's mind in this way.

**?**

1    What title was often given to Tantric teachers?
2    Why did Tantric Buddhists think it was important to have a *guru*?
3    What qualities does a *guru* need to have?
4    How many lifetimes does a Tantric Buddhist want to spend on becoming enlightened?

**HELPFUL MANTRAS**

An ancient Indian teaching which was followed by the Tantric Buddhists was that all physical things and mental states have a sound which corresponds to them. Thus, one way to understand the nature of the world and the mind was to learn and use the appropriate sounds. So, a meditation teacher who felt that one of his students needed to develop a particular quality would give that student a particular chant (*mantra*) to repeat. Often this *mantra* would be chanted aloud, but in the more advanced stages of practice the *mantra* would be repeated in the mind only.

**?**

1    What is a *mantra*?
2    How might a Buddhist argue that repeating certain sounds can have effects on your mental state?

One of the meanings of the word *mantra* is 'mind shelter'. Part of the Buddhist theory of meditation is that we can only focus our attention on one thing at a time. So if you are repeating a *mantra* you cannot be thinking about what might happen, or what someone else is doing. Repeating a *mantra* cuts out 'mental gossip'. Many Buddhists use *mantras* as prayers to keep evil influences away and to gain both spiritual and material benefits. Often a set number of repetitions of a particular *mantra* is performed in order to obtain a specific benefit.

A long time ago some clever Buddhists invented ways of multiplying the benefits gained from the repetition of *mantras*. They invented the prayer wheel and the prayer flag.

## Prayer Wheels

The prayer wheel is a cylinder, usually made of metal, with a *mantra* written all the way round the outside face. The cylinder is fixed to a central handle. A person holding the prayer wheel can make the cylinder spin by moving their wrist. Each complete spin counts as one repetition. By using a prayer wheel a person can get two repetitions in the time it takes to speak one.

## Prayer Flags

Tantric Buddhists have also been ready to use the forces of nature – wind power being one of the most popular. If a *mantra* were painted or embroidered on to a flag and the flag hoisted in the wind, every flutter could count as one repetition. This was getting the wind to do the work whilst the Buddhists received the benefits.

*Prayer wheels*

*Prayer flags*

1  Write down a popular meaning of the word *mantra*.
2  Explain one of the principles behind the use of *mantras*.
3  Explain what a Buddhist thinks about multiplying the benefits of *mantra* repetition by the use of prayer wheels and prayer flags.

## REVEALING RITUAL

Buddhist Tantric rituals are very symbolic. That means every item, every image, every sound and every gesture represents or stands for something else. Many of the rituals set out in Buddhist Tantric texts are written in code, what the Buddhists call 'twilight language'. Such code language served a number of purposes. First of all it helped to keep the teachings secret. If a person had not been taught the code, they could not understand the message.

Secondly, the code language would put off all those who were not serious about their practice. This was important because the Tantric practices were designed to liberate a person from rebirth in one lifetime. The early Buddhist scriptures report that at the time of the Buddha many people became *arhats* within a week of hearing him preach. At that time the differences between a *buddha* and an *arhat* were few. By the time of the later Mahayana, however, the attainments of the *arhats* were believed to fall far short of a *buddha*'s. It took many lifetimes to get from being an *arhat* to becoming a *buddha*. The Tantric teachers tried to change this. But, they said, the Tantric path was dangerous, there was the risk of going insane or ending up in one of the hells for thousands of years. Tantric techniques were, therefore, for the serious student only.

Thirdly, the symbols of the code were thought to have a power of their own. They could help a meditator to understand that it is our minds which determine how we make sense of the world. The Buddhist teaching of the truth of interdependence and interconnectedness is easily forgotten. This is because of our mind's tendency to think of things and people as realities in their own right. In other words, our tendency to label things gives them an individual identity which separates them from everything else. One of the ways people make this mistake is by dividing things into opposites such as good/bad, male/female, pure/impure. Buddhists call this 'dualistic thinking'. One of the main aims of Tantric ritual is to get rid of dualistic thinking.

So, if a person thought that certain foods or people were impure, the ritual might require them to eat the impure food or touch the impure person. This would help to free them from the restrictions that their view of things had imposed upon them.

In much Tantric art, sexual symbols are used to convey spiritual truth. Wisdom is often represented as a woman and skilful means as a man. The *bodhisattva* aims to unite these two. In Buddhist paintings this union is represented by a man and a woman in sexual intercourse. To those who are not initiated, who do not know the code, these images can be 'shocking'. To those who know, however, such symbols represent spiritual attainments. Other well-known symbols are the bell (*ghanta*), which represents compassion, and the thunderbolt (*vajra*), which represents wisdom.

> **?**
>
> 1 What do Buddhists call the code in which the Tantric texts were written?
> 2 Why is Tantric practice only for those who have been initiated?
> 3 What are the Tantric symbols for wisdom and compassion?
> 4 Explain in your own words the three reasons why Tantric Buddhist teachers used a code language.

Ghanta *and* vajra

# Chapter 13

# The End of Buddhism in India

After the time of Asoka, India once again became divided into a number of small kingdoms. Some of these were ruled by Hindu kings who did not support Buddhism. In such kingdoms, the lands given to the *sangha* by Asoka were taken back, and the *sangha* lost its financial support.

Both Mahayana and Tantric forms of Buddhism had more in common with Hindu systems than did the early forms of Buddhism. To many simple villagers, the heavenly *buddhas* and *bodhisattvas* of the Mahayana were not very different from the Hindu gods. Also, there were Hindu versions of Tantric practices as well as Buddhist ones. What is more, some of the *siddhas* were claimed as their own by Hindus as well as Buddhists.

Despite these setbacks, Buddhism remained a living force in many parts of India. But, from the seventh century CE onwards, it was attacked by members of another religion: Islam. These people invaded India again and again. Eventually, they conquered and occupied most of northern India.

The Buddhists were the most vulnerable to these attacks, partly because of the distinctive character of the monasteries and the monks. One saying of Muhammad, the prophet of Islam, was 'There shall be no monks in Islam', so the Muslim invaders tended to have a dislike for the Buddhist monks. Also, the statues and paintings in the monasteries were classed as 'idols' by the Muslims. The Muslim word for 'idol' was *budd*, an abbreviation of the Sanskrit word *buddha*. All 'idols' were either smashed or defaced by the Muslims. The Buddhist stress on non-violence meant that the monks did not stand up and defend themselves. Wherever the Muslims went, the Buddhists had to flee or die. The following story illustrates this well:

## The Warlord and the Monk

A Muslim warlord prided himself on having a frightening reputation. Whenever it was rumoured that he was near by, all the monks would run into the hills to hide. One day, however, the warlord's scouts returned from a monastery with disturbing news. Although most of the monks had fled to the hills, one of them had stayed behind. He was sitting in the middle of the monastery courtyard. Angry that news of his presence had not reduced the monk to terror, the warlord strode into the courtyard and right up to the monk. The monk stood up and bowed to the warlord who, drawing his sword, shouted in a loud voice, 'Don't you know who I am? I am a man who could take this sword and run it through your belly without blinking an eyelid.' In a gentle voice the monk replied, 'Don't you know who I am? I am a man who could let you run that sword through my belly without blinking an eyelid.'

The warlord realised that the monk was braver than he was, but he could not afford to lose face in front of his men so he stabbed the monk and ordered the monastery to be burned.

The warlord was prepared to kill for his religious beliefs; the monk was ready to die for his.

So it was that Buddhism ceased to exist in the land of its birth some time between 1100 and 1350 CE. By then, however, it had become well established in many other countries and all the major Indian Buddhist scriptures had been translated into other languages.

1    Why was Buddhism vulnerable to the attacks of Muslim invaders?
2    Do you think that being prepared to kill or die for your beliefs is a good thing? Discuss your answers.

# Part IV  BUDDHISM THROUGHOUT THE WORLD

<table>
<tr><td>

**Chapter**

**14**

</td><td>

# *Buddhist Missionaries and the Spread of Buddhism*

</td></tr>
</table>

**BUDDHISM NOT WANTED IN THE WEST**

Not all of the Buddhist missionaries sent out by the emperor Asoka were successful. This was particularly true in those countries which lay to the west of India.

A missionary travelling westwards from India came first of all to the kingdoms ruled by the followers of Alexander of Macedon which, at a later date, became parts of the Persian and Roman empires. Before the time of Alexander, the Persian Empire had adopted the Zoroastrian religion and it did so again when the empire was reunited under the Sassanian dynasty. In the early phase of its existence, the Roman Empire was tolerant of most religions and the Buddhists may have had some success, though there is little evidence for it. After the time of Constantine (who converted to Christianity in 337 CE), however, the Roman Empire became Christian. In the west, therefore, Buddhism had little effect on the lives of the people.

**BUDDHISM IS MORE SUCCESSFUL IN THE EAST**

To the east the Buddhists were much more successful. On the south-eastern route from India, Buddhism, in its Theravada form, was established in Sri Lanka, Burma, Thailand, Kampuchea (Cambodia) and Laos. In some form or other it still exists in these countries today. On the north-eastern route, Buddhism, in a variety of Mahayana forms, was established in Nepal, parts of Central Asia (now the northern parts of Afghanistan and Pakistan, southern USSR and western China), China, Korea, Japan and Vietnam. This last country was, in fact, missionised by both Theravada Buddhists from the south and Mahayana Buddhists from the north. Eventually, the northern form won the day and Vietnam became a mainly Mahayana Buddhist country. Later, Buddhism was taken to Tibet by Tantric Buddhists directly from India. From Tibet it then spread to Bhutan and Mongolia.

**?**

1   In which parts of the world were Buddhist missionaries not successful?
2   In which parts of the world were Buddhist missionaries successful?
3   Look at the chart on the next page and then write down:
   **a** the first five areas in which Buddhism was established;
   **b** the areas in which it still survives;
   **c** the area where Buddhism has existed for the longest period;
   **d** the area to which Buddhism has spread most recently.
4   Why did Buddhist missionaries not have much success in the west?

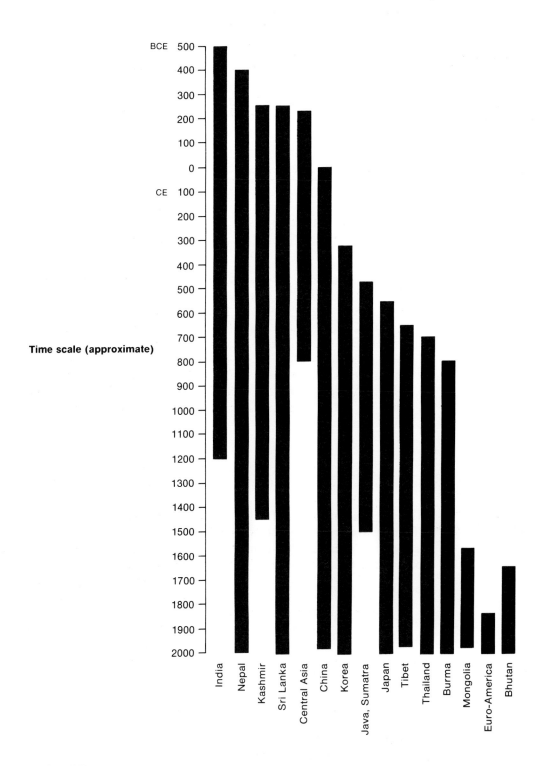

*The spread of Buddhism*

# The Southern Route: Theravada Buddhism

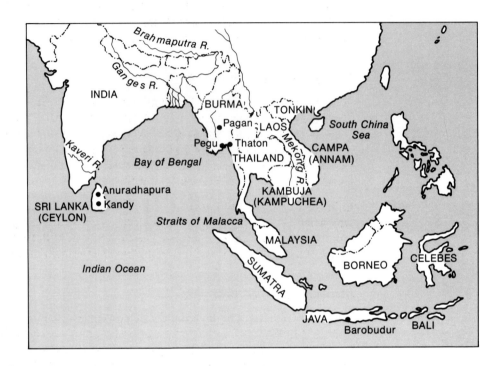

The southern route

## SRI LANKA

The first country south of India to which Buddhism was taken was Sri Lanka (formerly known in the West as the island of Ceylon). The dominant group on that island was the Sinhala clan, who were immigrants from northern India. The people of modern Sri Lanka are known as Sinhalese, after their first royal dynasty.

Buddhist tradition tells us that the Sinhalese king, Tissa, sent messengers to the emperor Asoka in India to request friendship between the two countries. Asoka's response was to send his son Mahendra/Mahinda, who was a Buddhist monk, with four others to the island. Tissa converted to Buddhism and soon afterwards most of the population followed him. Later, the monks were joined by nuns from India, so that Sinhalese women as well as men could be ordained.

The king donated a park in his capital of Anuradhapura to the monks and built a great monastery (*mahavihara*) within it. A shoot from the tree under which the Buddha gained enlightenment – the bodhi tree – was planted there. Since that time Buddhism has always been present in Sri Lanka and it is the religion of the majority of Sinhalese today. The form of Buddhism which has been most important in Sinhalese history is the Sthaviravada/Theravada.

**?**

1  Name the clan which ruled Sri Lanka when Buddhism arrived.
2  Name the leader of the Buddhist party which took Buddhism to the island and the king who was converted by him.
3  What is the old English name for Sri Lanka?
4  What is (a) a bodhi tree and (b) a *mahavihara*?

Throughout the history of Buddhism in Sri Lanka, the purity of the *sangha*, in other words the extent to which the monks live in the true spirit of the Buddha's teachings, has been under threat from two sources. These are the involvement of the monks in politics and their role as landowners.

## Monks as Landowners

Remember that in India the tradition of monks wandering around from place to place died out fairly soon after the death of the Buddha. Later, the tradition of giving land to the *sangha* developed. Kings were often the providers of such gifts. A central Buddhist teaching is that lay people earn merit by giving to the *sangha*. Usually they give food and basic clothing. When a king gives a gift, however, it is generally something rather more grand.

In Sri Lanka, kings often gave the Buddhist monks gifts of villages or reservoirs which supplied the villages with water. Sometimes such gifts were made to individual monks and they, in turn, passed them on to those who followed them. And so it was that, over time, the monks became the main landowners in Sri Lanka.

## Monks as Politicians

This new role of the *sangha* as landowner gave many monks a personal interest in politics. A traditional Buddhist idea was that the king supported the monks and the monks advised the king. The people, for their part, were ruled by the king and taught by the monks. In return, they obeyed the king and supported the monks. The relationship can be seen from the following two diagrams:

In reality things were much more complex. Once the different local *sanghas* were established as landowners, they were able to play a part in deciding who became king. The approval of the *sangha* came to be seen as essential for establishing a new king on the throne. Buddhism became a real power in the land.

## The King's Control

The king, for his part, had his own way of controlling the power of the *sangha*. In India, the emperor Asoka became involved in the affairs of the *sangha* and disrobed badly behaved monks. His example was followed by a number of Sinhalese kings who saw it as their duty to make sure that the *sangha* remained pure. Such purifications had political consequences. Monks who challenged the king's authority could be got rid of and any land or wealth owned by them could be claimed by the king.

## Buddhist Monks in Sri Lanka Today

Monks in Sri Lanka still play an active part in the political life of the island. They are also active in education and social work. However, all these activities run counter to the spirit of monastic discipline and many monks are criticised for their involvement in them. This issue of what are legitimate activities for a monk is likely to be one of the controversial elements in Buddhist debates over the next few decades.

1 What were the two main factors which threatened the purity of the *sangha* in Sri Lanka?
2 How did Sri Lankan kings try to control the power of various local *sanghas*?
3 Do you think the Buddha would have approved of monks becoming landowners and involving themselves in politics? Give reasons for your answers.

### The forest monks

Not all monks were landowners and politicians. Throughout most of Sinhalese history there have been monks who have tried to keep to the ancient lifestyle of meditator and ascetic. Kings involved in 'purification' campaigns would look to the example of such monks when deciding on the purity of landowning monks. However, the forest-dwelling lifestyle has never been popular. Out of a modern population of about 20 000 monks in Sri Lanka, only 600 or so are forest dwellers.

Since the growth of Western interest in meditation, Sri Lankan Buddhists have begun to take more notice of their forest traditions and the meditation techniques used in them. Nowadays many lay people practise meditation which, at one time, was an activity exclusive to the monks. This interest in meditation by lay people is a new development in the Buddhist world and is likely to achieve greater importance in the future.

1 Why do you think the life of the forest monk is less popular among the *sangha* than that of the village and town-dwelling monks?
2 Why do you think Buddhist lay people are becoming more interested in meditation?

### Traditions of ordination

When a Theravada Buddhist is ordained as a monk he is welcomed into the family of the Buddha. The monks who ordain him will be members of an ordination tradition or lineage (*nikaya*). A *nikaya* traces its history back to one of the great elders of former times and from him back to the Buddha. There are many *nikayas* in modern Sri Lanka, though most of them are associated with one of the three great *nikayas*: the Siyam Nikaya, founded in 1753 when monks from Thailand came to Sri Lanka to restore the higher ordination (in other words, the full ordination as a monk as distinct from the ordination for novicehood, *samanera*); the Amarapura Nikaya, founded in 1803 by monks who returned from Burma with the higher ordination; the Ramanna Nikaya, founded in 1865, which is also based on Burmese tradition. Monks attached to the last two *nikayas* can be identified by the fact that their robes cover both shoulders in the Burmese style.

**?**

1   What is the meaning of the term *nikaya*?
2   List the names and dates of foundation of the three great *nikayas* in present day Sri Lanka.
3   What does it mean to belong to a *nikaya*?
4   Which Sri Lankan monks wear their robes in the Burmese style?

**BURMA**

Buddhism has a long history in Burma. Although the Theravada form has tended to be strongest, the Mahayana and, later, the Tantric forms also enjoyed considerable success.

### The Early Years

The emperor Asoka sent Buddhist monks to the city of Thaton and Sinhalese documents report the attendance of Burmese Buddhist monks at a Sri Lankan ceremony during the second century BCE. From that time onwards Buddhism has flourished in Burma, though there have been several periods of setback and decline.

Right up to the eleventh century Buddhists had to compete with Hindus for the support of the Burmese people. However, during the reign of King Anawrahta (1040–77 CE), Theravada Buddhism received royal support and became the dominant religious tradition in Burma. Anawrahta's capital of Pagan became a centre of Buddhist culture and was known as a city of splendour. Thousands of pagodas, all beautifully built and elaborately decorated, were to be found within it.

*The Buddhist architecture of Burma*

## The Middle Period

In 1287 all the glories of the Pagan kingdom were brought to an end. Pagan was plundered by the Mongols under Kublai Khan and Burma was thrown into a state of division and decline. In the fifteenth century King Dhammaceti established a Buddhist kingdom with its capital at Pegu, just north of modern Rangoon. It was during the Pegu period that the king took the title of 'Ruler of the Sangha' (*sangha raja*) and began a tradition of state control over the monks. However, it was not until 1752 that Burma was reunited as one country and Buddhism was able to flourish throughout the nation.

Then, when the British took over in 1886, Buddhism again entered a period of decline, though in some ways the situation enabled it to put down some very strong roots among the Burmese population. During the period of British domination many Indians came to Burma and took over key government jobs. These outsiders were usually members of the Hindu, Christian or Muslim religions and so attachment to Buddhism became one way of remembering what it meant to be Burmese. The saying grew up that 'To be Burmese is to be a Buddhist.'

## The Modern Period

After the Second World War the government of Prime Minister U Nu wanted to bring Burma into the modern world and tried to unite the country by giving Buddhism a position of influence. The sixth Buddhist council, attended by monks from all Theravada countries, was held in Rangoon between 1954 and 1956. However, in 1962 General Ne Win, the Commander-in-Chief of the Burmese army, took over the government. Since that time Burma has been ruled by a military dictatorship.

Even with a military government Burma has remained a Buddhist country. In 1979 the minister of religion set up a congress. Its job was to create an organisation to control the entire Burmese *sangha*. Only those Burmese who accept the authority of the 33 '*sangha*-leaders' appointed by the organisation can be ordained as monks.

1    To which Burmese city did Asoka send missionaries?
2    Which king established Theravada as the main form of Buddhism in Burma?
3    For how long was Burma a disunited country after the Mongol invasion of 1287?
4    When and where was the sixth Buddhist council held?
5    In what year were the 33 '*sangha*-leaders' appointed to regulate the lives of Burmese monks?

## Monks and Lay Buddhists in Burma

The relationship between the monks and lay people of Burma today is probably closer than it is in Sri Lanka. One of the main reasons for this is that in Burma there is a strong tradition for most males to be ordained temporarily as a monk for at least one limited period, whereas in Sri Lanka monks are ordained for life. The tradition found in Burma is also common in other Theravada countries of South-East Asia: Thailand, Kampuchea and Laos. Many Burmese men are reordained each year at the beginning of the rainy season (July to October) and disrobe at the end of it, thus obtaining some experience of living in a monstery. The growth of lay meditation practice in Burma is largely a result of so many men having experienced monastic life.

Burmese monks spend much of their time in study as well as in meditation. The Abhidharma/Abhidhamma Pitaka of the Pali Canon (see Chapter 5) is, perhaps, the most popular book for study. Monks also teach the lay people, officiate at ceremonies such as funerals and recite the Paritra/Paritta texts (extracts from the scriptures believed to have protective powers) at special occasions.

The main role of the lay people, as it is in all Theravada countries, is to support the monks with basic necessities so that they can follow the religious life. In return for their support the lay people earn merit or 'good *karma*' which will help them in this life and, more importantly, help them to obtain a better rebirth next time round.

**?**

1   Why are the relationships between monks and lay people closer in Burma than in Sri Lanka?
2   What are the main activities of Burmese monks?
3   How do the lay people benefit from supporting the monks?
4   What difference does it make to relationships with lay people if monks are ordained for limited periods only?

## THAILAND, LAOS AND KAMPUCHEA

These three countries can be looked at together since the borders between them have changed many times during their histories. The fortunes of Theravada Buddhism have followed a similar pattern in all three countries up to modern times. The whole area was influenced by Indian traders and immigrants from the early centuries CE onwards. These Indians were both Hindus and Buddhists and they introduced the local populations to both religions. Only slowly did Theravada Buddhism become established as the national religion in all three countries.

### Thailand

In Thailand it was not until the end of the thirteenth century CE that Theravada Buddhism became the official religion. Before that it had competed with Mahayana forms of Buddhism and various kinds of Hinduism. There is still a fair degree of Hindu influence in modern Thailand, but it is at a popular level. Buddhism is the state religion and it is controlled by the state in many ways. In theory this position allows the monks to influence state policy. In practice, however, their role in national decision making is lessening as Thailand gradually takes on Western values which do not agree with Buddhist teaching.

### Kampuchea and Laos

Kampuchea became Theravadin at more or less the same time as Thailand. Buddhists of both countries maintained close contacts in the years which followed. In 1864 the discipline of the reformed community (*sangha*) of Thailand was introduced into Kampuchea. This reformed movement was started by a Thai king, who had also been a monk, in the first half of the nineteenth century. Its members observed a stricter code of discipline than the other monks.

In Laos, Theravada did not become the official religion until the middle of the fourteenth century. The Lao people changed Buddhism to fit their own needs so that it could exist alongside the traditional religion of Laos. It has prospered ever since that time.

## Modern Upheavals

During the Vietnam war the people of Thailand had quite a different experience from their neighbours in Kampuchea and Laos. The latter two countries became involved in the fighting and both were heavily bombed by the Americans. By contrast, Thailand became a major American base and a favourite centre of 'rest and recreation' for members of the American armed forces.

In Laos, the communist government which emerged after the war supported the *sangha* but continued and developed the tradition of state supervision and control. In recent interviews with members of the Western media Laotian leaders have said that they do not find Buddhism and Communism to be incompatible, although they do expect the monks to contribute to the development of the new communist state. The tradition of monastic retreat in the forest has come to an end in Laos, at least for the immediate future.

In Kampuchea, Theravada Buddhism has suffered more than anywhere else. When the Khmer Rouge communists came to power in 1975 most of the monks were murdered and Buddhism was more or less destroyed. Relief came in 1979 when the Vietnamese took over the country. Some monasteries were reopened but the roots of the religion, the monks, had been taken away. Now that the Vietnamese have left, the future of Kampuchea and its long tradition of Buddhism is again uncertain.

1  What status does Buddhism traditionally have in Thailand, Laos and Kampuchea?
2  In which of the three countries are Hindu beliefs and practices still found?
3  In what ways did the experience of each country's population differ during and after the Vietnam war?

## The Place of the *Sangha*

One feature of Buddhism in all these three countries is that it has been more formally involved with the government than has been the case in Sri Lanka or Burma. The traditional pattern has been this: the state has claimed the right to be involved in monastic affairs and the head of state has the power to appoint the head of the *sangha*.

The government's influence on Buddhism has led to the introduction of monastic examinations. This, in turn, has led to an emphasis on learning the Buddha's teachings rather than practising meditation, which is difficult to examine.

Discuss how it might be possible for a military regime and the *sangha* to co-exist.

*Monks studying in a university library*

## A Monk's Responsibilities

The role of the monk in these three countries has a number of aspects. These can be understood in terms of different responsibilities. First, he has a responsibility for his own spiritual progress; second, he has responsibilities connected with his monastery; finally, he has responsibilities to the lay people on whom he depends for the basics of life such as food and clothing.

A monk contributes to his own spiritual development by studying the scriptures, practising meditation and going on pilgrimages to Buddhist holy places. All monks are attached to a particular monastery. This is listed on the identity cards they receive when taking ordination. Once a month the monks of each monastery gather to recite the 227 rules under which they live. All resident monks are required to attend.

For lay people the main way of gaining merit is through the *sangha*. Since the monks are 'holy people' it is more meritorious to give to them than to anyone else. So the monks have a responsibility to make themselves available to receive gifts from the lay people. Usually these gifts are passed on to the monastery and held in common by all the monks. This prevents individual monks from becoming too attached to worldly goods.

Monks also conduct a range of ceremonies which are important to lay people, for example reciting selected Buddhist scriptures or taking a leading role at rites of passage. At funerals, the opportunity to remind people of the Buddha's teachings, particularly those concerned with impermanence, attachment and suffering, is always present. Marriage, for Buddhists, is not a sacrament. It is seen as desirable for a lay person who is unable to renounce the world, but is regarded as inferior to ordination. The role of monks at weddings is, therefore, usually rather minor.

**?**

1   List the three areas of a monk's responsibility.
2   Under how many rules do the monks live?
3   Why do lay people want to feed and clothe the monks? Write a letter explaining this to an English friend who thinks that monks are really just beggars pretending to be holy men.

# Chapter 16

# The Northern Route: China, Korea and Vietnam

**CHINA**

Buddhism in both its Hinayana and Mahayana forms was taken into China along the Silk Roads. The Sarvastivada school of Hinayana Buddhism dominated the northern route, and Mahayana Buddhism dominated the southern one (see p. 64). For a long time Buddhism made very little progress in China. Although there is some evidence for its presence in the first half of the first century CE, it did not become an important part of the Chinese religious scene until the period of disunity (311–589 CE). Most of the Buddhists in China up until that time were either foreigners or people of foreign descent.

The reasons for this slow progress are easy to see. Unlike the people in the countries on what we have called the southern route of Buddhist expansion, the Chinese possessed a long established and highly developed culture and civilisation before the arrival of Buddhism. If the Chinese Empire had not been broken up by invaders from the north, Buddhism would probably never have been accepted by the Chinese to the extent that it was. Buddhism is, in fact, the only non-Chinese religion ever to have become established in China. Even so, its history has not been one of steady gains but one of dramatic ups and downs.

## Other Religions

*Lao Tzu, Confucius and the Buddha*

When Buddhism was introduced into China two native religious traditions were already well established. These were Ju-chao or Confucianism, named after its founder Confucius (K'ung Fu-tzu), and Tao-chao or Taoism, the teaching about the Way (*Tao*).

## Confucianism

The Confucians stressed the importance of understanding human relations on the principle of order as seen in the movement of the stars. They were concerned with people's roles in society and the rules which control how people should behave. In other words, society, structure and order were the main concerns of Confucianism.

## Taoism

In many ways Taoism is the opposite of Confucianism. Rather than emphasising structure, the Taoists concentrated on process or change; rather than emphasising society, their concern was with the individual; rather than setting out the correct behaviour for every situation, the Taoists said that people should be adaptable. A favourite symbol of the Taoists was water. Water always goes around obstacles, it doesn't hurry unless the situation is right, but it always gets to its goal, the sea. Taoists taught that people should try to be like water and not be rigid in their attitudes or behaviour.

The Buddhists had quite a few things in common with the Taoists. Both groups thought that getting too involved with society was a hindrance to spiritual progress and both used meditation techniques to develop themselves. The Taoists also had a story that one of their greatest teachers, Lao Tzu, left China and travelled to the West. According to this story, Lao Tzu converted the Indians to Taoism – though the Indians called it Buddhism. And so the Taoists saw Buddhism as just a foreign version of Taoism. The Buddhists used many Taoist words when translating their scriptures into Chinese. This helped the Chinese to understand Buddhism, but it also changed Buddhist teachings in the process.

1 Which years are known as the period of disunity in Chinese history?
2 Why was it difficult for Buddhism to become established in China?
3 Name the two religions which Buddhism came into contact with in China and describe their teachings.
4 Imagine you are a Taoist and write a letter to an Indian friend explaining that the Buddha was really a Taoist.
5 If you think that this friend would not be convinced, write his letter of reply.

## The Period of Disunity: The Period of Success

Buddhism was first introduced into China during a period of relative stability, the period of the later Han dynasty (25–220 CE). When this dynasty collapsed in 220 CE, the country entered a time of upheaval and turmoil. In 311, the Mongols captured Lo-yang and then in 316 Ch'ang-an also fell. Most of the well-educated Chinese people, including learned Buddhist monks, moved to the south of the country and for more than 250 years China was divided into northern and southern kingdoms. These years were crucial for Buddhism. By the time unity was restored by the Sui dynasty in 589 CE, Buddhism was recognised as one of the three religions of China.

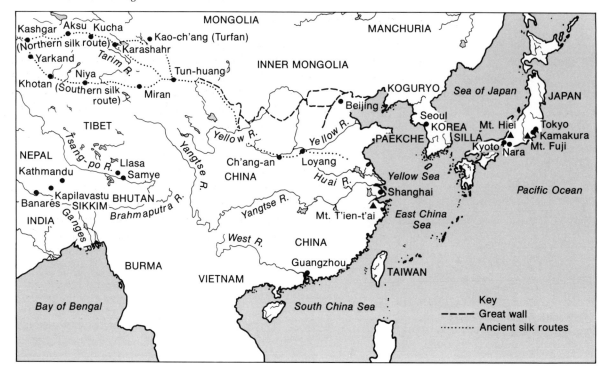

*The northern route*

## The Growing Popularity of Buddhism

During the Han dynasty the Buddhists of China spent much of their energy translating Buddhist texts into Chinese. In the period between the fall of the Han dynasty and the Mongols' capture of Lo-yang, Buddhist teachings began to be passed around among the native Chinese, including the upper classes. One of the main reasons for this was that the Chinese religions, Confucianism and Taoism, had not been able to provide good reasons for the changes which were taking place in Chinese society. Buddhism, with its teachings of impermanence and suffering, offered a way of understanding the situation and gave many Chinese people a sense of being able to cope.

In the southern kingdom, throughout the period of disunity, the Chinese acceptance of Buddhism increased. Many people from the upper classes converted to Buddhism and were able to explain it to others in a way that most Chinese could understand. At the same time there was the growing attraction of the monastery. Many cultured Chinese had lost most of their wealth in the move south and they could not find a place in the new administration. The Buddhist monasteries offered a place of retreat and study. Many Chinese gentlemen converted to Buddhism so they could go to these monasteries.

In the north, Buddhism was even more successful. There, the Mongol rulers supported Buddhism simply because it was not Chinese in origin. Texts were translated and temples were built. Monasteries were given land and the Chinese monks, like their fellows in Sri Lanka, became landlords.

## Not Everyone Liked Buddhism

As well as successes there were also setbacks and persecutions. As the rulers of the north began to accept Chinese culture, so they began to accept the criticisms of Buddhism made by the Chinese traditionalists. Such traditionalists argued that Buddhism was un-Chinese. First of all, the role of the monk in Buddhism contradicted the Chinese stress on the importance of family and the responsibilities to ancestors. Secondly, the fact that monks did not work meant that they were nothing more than parasites, living off the labour of others. Finally, the Buddhist claim that the monks did not have to accept the laws of the ruler meant that monasteries could easily become places for people who did not agree with the state and therefore encourage political revolution. In 574, the emperor Wu said that Buddhist monasteries, scriptures and images were to be destroyed, monks and nuns disrobed, and the wealth of the monasteries confiscated. Fortunately for the Buddhists the persecution was short lived, as the emperor Wu died in 578.

**?**

1   For about how long was China divided into northern and southern kingdoms?
2   What were the main reasons for Buddhism becoming established in the south?
3   What were the main reasons for Buddhism becoming established in the north?
4   In what ways were Buddhists said to be un-Chinese?

## The Triumph of Buddhism in China

*An out-of-the-way Buddhist monastery*

Wu's successor was sympathetic to Buddhism, as was Yang Chien who founded the Sui dynasty in 581. Yang Chien made himself ruler by force. He needed a belief system which would help him to unite the people. He chose Buddhism. In 589 he conquered the southern kingdom and reunified China. The following years were some of the most successful for Buddhism.

Yang Chien modelled himself on the Indian emperor Asoka. He rebuilt the monasteries and temples, reinstated the monks and nuns, and sent missionary groups throughout the Empire. For the next 300 years Buddhism became the main religion in China.

Although they had brought together and strengthened the Chinese Empire, both Yang Chien and his son Kuang, who succeeded him, were impatient and extravagant. They tried to do too much too quickly and damaged the economy of the country. In 618 Kuang was assassinated and the Sui dynasty was replaced by the T'ang.

The T'ang emperors tended to prefer Confucianism, but they also supported Buddhism and encouraged a sense of tolerance on religious matters. The great Chinese Buddhist schools, almost all Mahayana, flourished during this period.

**?**

1    Which dynasty replaced the Sui in 618 CE?
2    Why do you think the great Chinese Buddhist schools were Mahayana?

## Major Buddhist Schools in China

Chinese Buddhists were faced with a problem that their fellows in India had not had to face. The great number of Buddhist scriptures that they had translated were from various time periods in Buddhism's history and often represented the views of different Buddhist schools. They were, nevertheless, all presented as the word of the Buddha.

In response to the large number of scriptures, some groups selected particular texts, which they thought presented the highest teaching of the Buddha. Other groups preferred to work out ways of classifying the scriptures, making sure that their preferred texts were given the highest place.

### Selected scriptures
Examples of the first kind of school are the Pure Land school (Ching-t'u), the Nature of Things school (Fa-hsiang) and the Three Treatises school (San-lun). These were based on the Pure Land (Sukhavati) Sutras, the writings of the Yoga Practice (Yogacara) teachers and the writings of the Middle Position (Madhyamaka) teachers respectively (see pp. 69 and 74–7 of Chapter 11).

### Classified scriptures
Most famous of the schools which preferred to classify all the Buddhist scriptures are the T'ien-t'ai (named after the mountain on which its founder lived) and the Hua-yen (Flower Garland) schools. It was the founder of the T'ien-t'ai school, Chih-i, who first developed the system of classification known as *p'an chiao* (dividing the teachings into periods). He argued that there were five periods of the Buddha's teaching. In each of these he taught a different doctrine according to the ability of his audience to understand.

1 What problems did the Chinese face when they tried to make sense of all the Buddhist scriptures?

2 Describe the two ways in which Chinese Buddhist schools dealt with the number of scriptures and the differences in their teachings.

3 Link each of the schools listed below with the appropriate scripture:

San-lun        Sukhavati texts
Fa-hsiang     Yogacara texts
Ching-t'u      Madhyamaka texts

### Distinctly Chinese

The T'ien-t'ai and Hua-yen schools did not exist in India. They are Chinese creations, even though they are based on Indian texts. Both schools reflect a typical Chinese concern for order. Another famous Chinese school which did not exist in India is the Meditation school (Ch'an, or Zen in Japanese). The teachings of this school reflect another typical Chinese concern, that of practicality. It is also a good example of a school which emphasised the Chinese concern for family tradition and history.

The Meditation school stressed that practice was more important than theory and that the teaching should be passed on from one living person (a master) to another (a pupil) directly. Scriptures were, therefore, unnecessary. The Meditation school also stressed the importance of belonging to a 'lineage' of teachers. If Chinese Buddhist monks left their families in order to live in a monastery they did not abandon family traditions altogether for they became part of a spiritual family with its own tradition of venerable ancestors. This was one way in which the Meditation school responded to the criticisms of the Chinese traditionalists. Another way was by requiring monks to work. A famous saying in the monasteries of the Meditation school was 'One day no work, one day no food'. These are two examples of how the Meditation school adapted itself to the Chinese situation better than did most of the other Chinese Buddhist schools.

1 List three Chinese Buddhist schools which did not exist in India.

2 In what ways did the Meditation school try to avoid the criticisms made against Buddhism by Chinese traditionalists?

## The Decline of Buddhism in China

Towards the end of the T'ang dynasty there were around 5000 monasteries, 40 000 small temples and shrines and some 270 000 fully ordained monks and nuns in China. Much land and a great deal of wealth was owned by these Buddhist institutions. Not surprisingly, they attracted considerable attention from the Chinese rulers. After the great civil war of the mid-eighth century, the rulers were always on the lookout for ways of finding wealth. So, influenced by the Confucian traditionalists, they took it from the Buddhists.

In 842 CE the hammer fell. Buddhism was not outlawed, but much of the land and treasure owned by monasteries and temples was confiscated. In 845 most of the monasteries were destroyed and the monks and nuns were forced to return to lay life. Buddhism never regained the position it had achieved under the Sui and early T'ang dynasties.

Imperial persecution was not, however, the only force which contributed to Buddhism's decline in China. The Confucians had taken many Buddhist ideas that were popular among the Chinese and woven them into their own system of philosophy. The result was called Neo-Confucianism.

Another contribution to Buddhism's decline in China was the fact that new Buddhist teachings were no longer coming from India as Buddhism was declining there.

### Survivors

After the collapse of the T'ang dynasty in 906 CE, China entered an unsettled period until the founding of the Sung dynasty in 960. By this time most of the Buddhist schools which had flourished under the Sui and T'ang dynasties had disappeared. Only those which had been able to adapt to the Chinese situation survived. The two main survivors were the Pure Land school (Ch'ing-tu) and the Meditation school (Ch'an).

In terms of numbers, Buddhism was not too badly affected, but there was a clear drop in the quality of the people who came forward for ordination. So the Buddhism of this period became mainly a popular religion.

## The Modern Period

During the modern period, since 1911, a number of attempts to revive Buddhism have been made. Noteworthy among these was the founding of the Chinese Buddhist Association in 1929. Overall, however, the picture has been one of decline. In 1949 the Chinese communists came to power. Shortly afterwards the monasteries were, once again, deprived of their land and the monks and nuns made to work for their living. Many people predicted that Buddhism would disappear from China altogether.

### Buddhism and political freedom

Buddhism played little part in Chinese life under Mao Zedong, but under the religious freedom introduced by his successor, Deng Xiaoping, many Buddhists have declared themselves in public. Most of them are from the older generation. If there is an increase in political freedom in China, more Chinese might well choose to follow Buddhism. It is, after all, an international religion and has influenced their country for nearly 2000 years.

?

1    Which Chinese Buddhist schools best survived the persecution of 842–5 CE?
2    Despite the persecutions, the number of Buddhists in China did not fall very much. In what way, then, can Buddhism be said to have declined after the T'ang dynasty?
3    As the fate of Buddhism is clearly affected by political events, should Buddhists take an active role in politics? What do you think the Buddha would have said?

## KOREA  The Early Phase

In the early period of its history Korea was greatly influenced by Chinese ideas. It was Buddhists who took Chinese culture to Korea and introduced the Koreans to the Chinese script. Until 688 CE, Korea was divided into three kingdoms: Koguryo in the north, Paekche in the south-west and Silla in the south-east (see the map on p. 96). Each of the three kingdoms adopted Buddhism as the official religion before the country was unified by the kingdom of Silla in 688. Buddhism was a major influence in creating a sense of Korean unity.

### Chinese influence

The Silla rulers of Korea followed the example of the Chinese T'ang dynasty. They used Confucianism for political and state arrangements but preferred Buddhism for religious teachings. All the main Chinese Buddhist schools flourished, though the Meditation school (called Son in Korean) was by far the most successful. Among the common people it was, as in China, the Pure Land teaching which was most popular.

The Koryo dynasty replaced the Sillan in 918. Under these rulers Buddhism was at its most successful in Korea. Many monasteries were built and Buddhist themes showed strongly in the artistic life of the country.

1  Name the three ancient kingdoms of Korea.
2  In which year were they unified?
3  Which Chinese Buddhist school was most successful in Korea? What reasons can you give for its success?

### Decline and persecution

In 1392 the Koryo dynasty was succeeded by the Yi. Following the example of the Ming rulers in China, who came to power in 1368, the Yi rulers gave their support to Confucianism. From that time until the end of the nineteenth century, when the Japanese took control of Korea, the story of Buddhism was one of decline. State support was withdrawn and the various Buddhist schools were forced to join together and form seven schools. These were later combined to make just two. Much later, in 1935, this division was done away with and all Korean Buddhists became part of the new Chogye school. From 1623 until 1895 Buddhist monks were even prevented from entering the capital.

### Japanese influence

Under the Japanese the fortunes of Buddhism began to improve. Monks were allowed back into the capital and the Buddhists received Japanese help to re-establish their religion. Even so, the Korean and Japanese Buddhists did not always agree with each other. The Koreans followed the Buddhist rules quite strictly and did not allow monks to marry. The Japanese preferred a less strict approach and in 1908 gave permission for Korean monks to marry. This issue of married monks versus celibate monks is still a source of disagreement among Korean Buddhists.

1  Under which dynasty did Buddhism rise to the height of its prestige in Korea?
2  Under which dynasty did Buddhism suffer severe persecution in Korea?
3  What was the main point of disagreement between Korean and Japanese Buddhists?

**4**     Imagine you are a group of Buddhists. Debate whether monks should be allowed to marry.

## The Modern Period

After the Second World War, the period of Japanese rule came to an end. Korea, however, was divided into two separate states: the communist north and the so-called democratic south. In both of these states land reforms, which took wealth away from the Buddhists, were introduced. Since then Buddhism has virtually ceased to exist in North Korea. In the south, on the other hand, the government paid compensation to the monasteries for the land they had lost. This money was invested and now the Buddhists have enough money to make sure that their organisation survives.

### Married monks

Despite its financial security, Buddhism in South Korea is not without its problems. In 1954 the government supported the celibate monks and ordered all those who were married to leave the monasteries. Eventually, after eight years of bitter arguments, a compromise was reached. Married monks were allowed to stay in the *sangha* and hold various offices within its organisation. They were not, however, allowed to become the head of the Korean Buddhist organisation.

### Towards the future

Since the war, South Korean Buddhists have become more socially active than at any time in the past, particularly in the field of education. Slowly Buddhism is regaining ground in South Korea. New monasteries are being built and ancient ones restored. Today, there are about six million Buddhists in South Korea and the numbers are growing. It looks as though Buddhism is entering a new and positive phase in Korea.

**1**     In which part of Korea does Buddhism seem to have disappeared?
**2**     In which social sphere have South Korean Buddhists become particularly active?
**3**     Which office can married monks not hold in the modern Buddhist organisation of Korea?
**4**     About how many Buddhists are there in Korea today?

**VIETNAM**     The country now known as Vietnam was, from the second century CE until 939 CE, divided into two culture zones. The north, known as Tonkin, came under the influence of China; the south, divided into Campa and Funan, was mainly influenced by the cultures of India and the Indianised states of Thailand, Kampuchea and Laos.

## The South

From the third to the ninth centuries CE, Theravada Buddhism was well supported in the south. However, in the later part of that period it had to compete with Mahayana and Tantric forms of Buddhism as well as with different kinds of Hinduism. When Buddhism started to receive royal support in the ninth century it was the Mahayana form that had become popular.

## The North

In the north, Tonkin was the southernmost province of the Chinese Empire and the ruling classes followed Chinese customs. During the period of disunity in China (see p. 95), Buddhist missionaries were able to establish their religion in Tonkin. The most successful Chinese Buddhist school was the Meditation school (called Thien by the Vietnamese). Unlike the Chinese monks of this school, the Vietnamese ones played an active part in the development of their country's culture. The other main Buddhist influence in the north was the Pure Land school, which was the most popular form of Buddhism in the villages. When Vietnam became independent of China in 939 CE, this pattern of Thien in the monasteries and Pure Land in the villages continued to exist.

## Persecution

From the end of Chinese rule to the fall of the Tran dynasty in 1400 Buddhism flourished in Vietnam. After that, however, it suffered from persecution by the government, which modelled its administration on Chinese lines and turned to Confucian ideas in an attempt to become more powerful. Later, the Buddhists suffered at the hands of French colonialists and the Roman Catholic missionaries who came with them. When Vietnam was divided politically into north and south, the communists in the north attempted to stamp out all religions, including Buddhism. In the south the puppet governments established by the French and then the Americans refused Buddhists a say in the running of the country. They were too close to the Vietnamese people to be trusted. Since the victory of the Vietnamese over the Americans, the policy of religious suppression has been extended from the north to the south. It now seems unlikely that Buddhism will survive in Vietnam.

**?**

1 Name the three areas which came to form the country now known as Vietnam.
2 Which Buddhist tradition was most successful in the south?
3 Which Buddhist school was most popular in the Vietnamese villages?
4 What is the Vietnamese name for the Meditation school?
5 Which other religions contributed to the decline of Buddhism in Vietnam?

<table>
<tr><td>

**Chapter**

**17**
</td><td>

# *The Northern Route: Japan*
</td></tr>
</table>

## The Six Periods of Japanese History

A convenient way of understanding how Buddhism developed in Japan is to divide its history into six periods. Each period, except the first and the last, links with the location of the capital city. The six periods are listed below.

1  **The early period**   capital located in the city of the ruling family.

2  **The Nara period**   capital located at Nara.

3  **The Heian period**   capital located at Heian-Kyo (now called Kyoto).

4  **The Kamakura period**   capital located at Kamakura.

5  **The Edo period**   capital located at Edo (now called Tokyo).

6  **The modern period**   capital located at Tokyo.

**THE EARLY PERIOD (538–710 CE)**

In 538 CE, the Korean king of Paikche sent a mission to the Japanese emperor (*mikado*) asking for help in his wars with the other Korean kingdoms. The mission took with them, as gifts for the emperor, a gold-plated bronze image of the Buddha, some Buddhist scriptures and a letter recommending the new religion. The emperor decided to give Buddhism a try, though he soon rejected it when plague broke out in the country. However, the seed was sown and within a year the Japanese people began turning to Buddhism. Within 50 years it was recognised and supported by the emperor.

### Prince Shotoku

The most outstanding Japanese figure of the early period was Prince Shotoku. His aunt, the empress Suiko, was a keen Buddhist and ordained as a nun shortly after she came to the throne. She appointed her nephew Shotoku to rule as regent in her place. During his period of office (592–621), Shotoku made Buddhism the state religion in all but name.

#### A 17-article constitution

Taking his inspiration from the teaching of the Buddha, Shotoku drew up a 17-article constitution, the first words of which are: 'Harmony is more valuable than anything else.' He stressed tolerance and compassion as important qualities, encouraged his subjects to be honest and humane with each other, and required his officials to deal justly with his people. He also built many temples, commissioned works of art, supported monks in their study of the scriptures and encouraged scholars and monks to visit China for inspiration.

When the capital moved to Nara in 710 CE, Buddhism was the religion most supported by the imperial court.

**?**

1    What were the gifts sent by the king of Paikche to the emperor of Japan?
2    What was happening in China and Korea at the time when Buddhism was introduced into Japan?
3    In whose place did Prince Shotoku rule Japan?
4    Compare the activities of Shotoku with those of Asoka. How similar were they?

## THE NARA PERIOD (710–84 CE)

In the years after the death of Prince Shotoku, Buddhism continued to receive support from the Japanese rulers. There was, however, a price to pay. The monks and nuns had to pray for the welfare of the nation and be obedient to state officials. Such behaviour is not allowed by the Buddhist monastic code, because, according to Buddhist teaching, monks and nuns have a higher status than worldly rulers. Japanese rulers, however, have never accepted that a religion should be above state control, and monks and nuns who failed to do what the rulers wanted were punished.

The government exercised further control over the Buddhists by ruling that only monks who were ordained at a recognised ordination ceremony would be accepted by the state. At first there was only one recognised ordination centre, at the Todaji temple, though two others were established shortly afterwards.

### An Upper-Class Religion

Very few of the Japanese Buddhists from the Nara period went out to teach the population. Buddhist teachings and practices, as well as the various elements of Chinese culture which went along with them, were only available to the upper classes and state officials. The Buddhism of this period tended to be rather literary and scholastic.

### Support from the Emperor Shomu

Perhaps the greatest supporter of Buddhism during the Nara period was the emperor Shomu, who reigned from 724 to 749 CE. He had a monastery and a nunnery built in every province. The main duties of the monks and nuns in these places were to pray and perform rituals for the benefit of the nation. In the capital at Nara, Shomu built two large temples which acted as headquarters for the provincial monasteries and nunneries. The Todaji (Great Temple of the East) controlled the monasteries, whilst the Hokkeji (Temple of the *Dharma* Blossom) controlled the nunneries. The great hall of the Todaji is still the largest wooden building in the world. It was rebuilt twice after devastating fires in 1180 and 1567. It contains the largest metal image in Japan, a 14.25-metre-high bronze figure of the Buddha Vairocana (the main *buddha* in the Avatamsaka Sutra) which weighs 380 tons. (See the photograph on p. 106.)

*The Todaji*

## Japanese Buddhism Changes

Towards the end of the Nara period we see changes in Japanese Buddhism. A growing number of lay Buddhist preachers began wandering around Japan, introducing simple forms of the teachings to ordinary people. These preachers were soon given the title of 'holy men' (*hijiri*). They were critical of the established schools which, they said, were of little help to the people.

There was also a closer relationship developing between Buddhism and the native Japanese religion of Shinto. Shrines dedicated to the Shinto gods (*kami*) were built in the grounds of Buddhist temples, and the gods were believed to protect the temples.

1   What did the Buddhist monks and nuns have to do for the state in return for government support?
2   Which groups of people had most contact with Buddhism during the Nara period?
3   Name the temple whose great hall is the largest wooden building in the world.
4   What were the main changes taking place in Buddhism towards the end of the Nara period?
5   Which features of Nara Buddhism would the Buddha have been pleased with and which would he have been displeased with? Give reasons for your answers.

## THE HEIAN PERIOD (782–1192 CE)

In 782 CE, the emperor Kwammu moved the capital from Nara to Nagaoka. He was, however, unhappy with the new site and so, in 783, he moved it once more, this time to Heian-Kyo (the capital of peace and tranquillity). In time this name was shortened to Kyoto (the capital).

Although the new capital was built in a Chinese style, the Heian period marks the beginnings of the process by which Japan became less dependent on China for its cultural inspiration. The move to the new capital was probably an expression of the emperor's wish to be free of the influence of the Buddhist monks in Nara. In fact, it achieved much more than that, it also freed Japanese Buddhists from the restrictions of the Nara-controlled ordination requirements.

---

## Two Important Buddhist Monks

Two figures stand out above all others in the history of Buddhism during the Heian period. They are Saicho and Kukai.

### Saicho

Saicho (767–822) built a small monastery on mount Hiei, north-east of Heian, in 788. There he studied Mahayana teachings, particularly those of the Chinese T'ien-t'ai school (see p. 98). In 783 the emperor took part in a ceremony at the Hiei monastery for the purification of the site on which the new capital was to be built. The emperor was pleased with Saicho and in 804 sent him to China for a year's study.

On his return to Japan, Saicho developed his own version of T'ien-t'ai (called Tendai in Japanese). This included parts taken from the Meditation school, the Discipline school and the Tantric school. He also set up an extremely strict programme of training for the monks who came to study under him. They had to spend 12 years on mount Hiei in study and meditation. This training won great respect for the monks of the Tendai school. Saicho also tried to get permission to ordain monks on mount Hiei, but the monks of Nara objected. After his death, however, permission was finally granted and the old rules on ordination were changed.

### Kukai

Kukai (774–835) was a younger contemporary of Saicho. In the words of one scholar, 'Whereas Saicho was a good monk and a fine teacher, Kukai . . . was a genius.'* During the years 804 to 806 he studied Tantric Buddhism in China. When he returned to Japan in 806 he founded the True Word school (called Shingon in Japanese). Kukai was a great writer and philosopher and was highly honoured by the emperor. In 816 he founded a monastery on mount Koya and many disciples studied under him. For a time the Shingon school became even more popular than the Tendai school.

---

## Japanese Buddhism Divides into Small Sects

Towards the end of the Heian period Japanese Buddhism, reflecting the lack of unity in the Japanese state, started to break up into many small sects. The Buddhist teachings and practices developed by Saicho proved to be too difficult for many Tendai monks. Large numbers of them started to look for simpler versions of Buddhism.

---

*R. Robinson and W. Johnson, *The Buddhist Religion* (Wadsworth, 3rd edn 1982, p. 201).

At this time, the teaching of Mappo (the view that the time of decline in the power and purity of the *Dharma* as predicted by the Buddha was here) captured the minds of many Japanese. The government could not hold the country together and regional aristocratic families became more independent and powerful.

1   Name the two most outstanding Buddhist monks of the Heian period and the mountains on which they established their monasteries.
2   Name the schools these monks introduced into Japan.
3   List the reasons why Buddhism started to break up towards the end of the Heian period. Which of these was the most important? Discuss your answers.

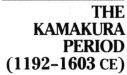

## THE KAMAKURA PERIOD (1192–1603 CE)

The rise to power of the provincial aristocracy which took place towards the end of the Heian period led to many wars between rival families. These conflicts were brought to an end in 1185 when Yoritomo Minamoto defeated his family's main opponents, the Taira clan. In 1192 he established the capital at Kamakura and took the title Shogun, military ruler. In theory the Shoguns were the emperor's regents, in practice they were the actual rulers.

## Wandering Buddhist Preachers

During the Kamakura period Buddhism became a much more popular religion with the Japanese people. This was due to the growth in the number of wandering Buddhist preachers and the formation of typically Japanese schools of Buddhism. One fifteenth-century writer claimed that about a third of the Japanese population were wandering preachers. This is almost certainly an exaggeration, but it was probably true that such preachers were becoming more and more common in towns and villages. The three main schools of Buddhism in this period were the Pure Land schools (Jodo Shu and Jodo Shinshu), the Meditation school (Zen) and the Nichiren school (named after its founder, Nichiren).

1   What was the title taken by Yoritomo Minamoto when he established the capital at Kamakura in 1192?
2   Why did Buddhism become a more popular religion during the Kamakura period?
3   List the three schools of Japanese Buddhism which became influential in the Kamakura period.

## The Pure Land Schools (Jodo Shu and Jodo Shinshu)

Teaching about the Pure Land was introduced into Japan by the Tendai school. For most Tendai monks, however, this teaching was just a small part of the Mahayana Buddhist world-picture. Even so, a few Tendai monks gave the Pure Land teaching a special emphasis: Kuya (903–72) danced in the street and sang popular songs about Amida Buddha (Amitabha – see p. 75), and Genshin (942–1017) wrote a widely read text in which he argued that the Pure Land path was the best since it was open to all people, monk or lay, saint or sinner.

### Chanting and trust

Honen (1133–1212) was another Tendai monk who emphasised the Pure Land teaching. He was greatly influenced by the teaching of Mappo (see above). He said that the only way to make spiritual progress in the present evil age was by chanting 'Hail Amida Buddha' (*Namu Amida Butsu*) and by trusting in the power of Amida. He called his school the 'Pure Land Teaching' (Jodo Shu). His disciple, Shinran (1173–1263), went even further. He said that the power of Amida's vow (i.e. that all who hear his name will be born in the Pure Land – see p. 75) meant that everyone was already guaranteed a place in the Pure Land. The only thing that prevented people receiving Amida's grace was their lack of faith. Shinran called his school the 'True Pure Land Teaching' (Jodo Shinshu).

**?**

1   Which Buddhist school introduced the Pure Land teaching into Japan?
2   Name the founder of the Jodo Shu school.
3   Name the founder of the Jodo Shinshu school.
4   In what ways did the teachings of these schools differ from each other?
5   Write down three reasons why Buddhists might find it hard to trust in the power of Amida's vow. Discuss your answers.

## The Meditation Schools (Rinzai Zen and Soto Zen)

Like the Pure Land teaching, meditation was just a part of the teachings of other schools. In the same way that Honen and other Tendai monks simplified Buddhism by emphasising the power of Amida's grace, Eisai and Dogen placed meditation at the centre of Buddhist practice.

### Eisai and Rinzai Zen

When he returned from a visit to China in 1191, Eisai (1141–1215) established the Rinzai Meditation school. Rinzai Zen is famous for its use of the *koan* as a form of meditation. A *koan* is a verbal trick aimed at awakening the mind. One of the most well known *koans* is 'What is the sound of one hand clapping?' There is no straightforward answer to this question, nor is it meant to be. In common with many other Buddhist schools, the Rinzai teachers taught that the ordinary working of a person's mind is what prevents him or her from awakening to the true nature of things. The idea behind the *koan* is that because the question has no answer a person who tries to find one will eventually come to a point where ordinary thinking just stops. At this moment the meditator has the chance to see things as they really are.

Eisai's no-fuss, very strict form of Buddhism was popular with the military rulers who saw it as a religion suitable for the warrior class (*samurai*). His training for keeping one's mind on what is happening in the present moment was helpful to the *samurai*. If their minds started to wander in battle there was a good chance they would be killed. So meditation training and warrior training were seen to fit together well. The link between meditation and martial skills eventually gave rise to the various Japanese 'ways' (*do*), such as *kendo* (the way of the sword) and *kyudo* (the way of archery).

Eisai is also famous for bringing tea-seeds from China and introducing the tea ceremony.

### Dogen and Soto Zen

Dogen (1200–53) was a student of Eisai's chief disciple. Like many great Japanese Buddhist masters before him, Dogen visited China where he studied from 1223 to

1227. On his return to Japan he tried to avoid becoming involved in the politics of the day and so moved into a small rural monastery to teach *zazen* (sitting meditation). This practice was so popular that he had to move to larger premises several times.

*Zazen* practice is another way of keeping the mind focused on the present moment. Only in the present can awakening take place, only in the present can things be seen as they really are.

Dogen's school is called Soto Zen. Another Zen school, the Obaku, was introduced into Japan in the fifteenth century but, despite linking its teaching with that about the Pure Land, it never became as popular as the Rinzai and Soto schools.

1  Name the founders of the Rinzai and Soto schools of Zen Buddhism.
2  Which Zen master introduced the tea ceremony into Japan?
3  Explain in your own words what you understand by the words *koan* and *zazen*.
4  What attracted the military rulers to Zen Buddhism?
5  In what ways do the techniques of Zen Buddhism overlap with those of early Buddhism?

## The Nichiren School (Nichiren Shu)

The Nichiren school is the only Buddhist school named after the person who founded it. Like many other famous Japanese Buddhists, Nichiren (1222–82) studied Tendai teaching on mount Hiei. He accepted the Tendai view that the Lotus Sutra represents the highest form of Buddhist teaching. He did not, however, feel that in the age of Mappo the complete *sutra* needed to be studied. For him, the words 'Salutations to the Lotus Sutra' (*Namu myo-ho-ren-ge-kyo*) contained the essence of the entire text. Nichiren went on to develop his own version of what he understood as the true Buddhism. It has three main parts:

● **the *daimoku***   the chant of *namu myo-ho-ren-ge-kyo*;

● **the *honzon***   a diagram which represents the entire universe;

● **the *kaidan***   the shrine where the *honzon* is placed. A physical *honzon* can be kept in the home but, according to Nichiren, the true *honzon* lies in the heart of the believer.

Nichiren taught that only those who worship the Buddha Sakyamuni by means of the *daimoku*, *honzon* and *kaidan* could be saved. He also claimed that other forms of Buddhism were corrupt and the cause of all Japan's problems. Not surprisingly, he found himself in conflict with other Buddhists, who were outraged by his attitude.

1  Which scripture did Nichiren think contained the highest Buddhist teaching?
2  Explain in your own words what the *daimoku*, *honzon* and *kaidan* are.
3  Why did Nichiren come into conflict with other Buddhists?
4  What do you think the Buddha would have said about Nichiren's teachings? Give reasons for your answer.

## Unity Lost and Restored

In the later part of the Kamakura period the unity established by the Minamoto Shoguns began to break up and Japan entered a period of warfare between the rival great families. During this time many Buddhist monasteries took an active part in political manoeuvring, often using the troops they employed in order to get their own way. Eventually, however, the country was reunited under a powerful military leader, Oda Nobunaga. He decided to discipline the Buddhists who had interfered in political affairs. In 1571 he destroyed the Tendai monastery (which by then had become a fortress) on mount Hiei; in 1580 he destroyed the Jodo Shinshu fortress at Osaka. His successor, Hideyoshi, destroyed the Shingon fortress at Negoro in 1585. By the beginning of the Edo period (1603), all the fortified monasteries had been destroyed or brought under state control.

**?**

**1**  Link the schools listed below with the place where their main fortified monasteries were located:

Tendai          Osaka
Jodo Shinshu    Negoro
Shingon         Kyoto

**2**  Whereas the Indian Buddhist monks were prepared to die for their religious beliefs when they were attacked by the Muslims, the Japanese monks hired soldiers to fight for them and protect them. What does this tell you about the Buddhism of the two countries?

## THE EDO PERIOD (1603–1868 CE)

Japan was reunited under a single government by Hideyoshi's successor Tokugawa Ieyesu (1542–1616). He gained control over the country in 1600 after defeating his enemies in battle. In 1603 he moved the capital to Edo and took the title Shogun. Ieyesu, and the Tokugawa Shoguns who followed him, held Japan together by imposing strict rules on the entire population. Contact with other countries, including China, was carefully controlled and the close relationship between the Zen Buddhists and the government was brought to an end. The Tokugawa rulers thought that Neo-Confucianism was the best philosophy for the state to follow, since it stressed social responsibility more than Buddhism did. All Buddhist monks had to be registered and they had to obtain permission from the government to build a new monastery or found a new school.

## Everyone Registers as a Buddhist

Under the Tokugawa rulers Japan was divided into parishes (*danka*). Every member of the population had to register themselves at the monastery of their parish. Thus, everyone in Japan became a Buddhist, in name at least. They were thereby guaranteed a Buddhist funeral. In this way the Buddhists were given the opportunity to spread their teachings among the ordinary people.

## Government Support for Some Types of Buddhism

Some monks were encouraged by the government to take up scholarly pursuits, such as translating texts and writing histories and biographies, which would keep them out of politics. Some also took up one or more of the ways (*do*), such as swordfighting, archery and flower arranging. Certain forms of Buddhism were, however, not tolerated by the government and had to go underground. Pure Land and Nichiren Buddhism were the two main schools to be outlawed by the Tokugawa rulers.

**?**

1    Which military leader reunified Japan in 1600?
2    Which philosophy did he and his successors regard as the most suitable for the government to adopt?
3    How and why did Buddhism suffer and benefit under the Tokugawa Shoguns?
4    Why do you think the Tokugawa rulers did not like the teachings of the Pure Land and Nichiren schools? Discuss your answers.

## THE MODERN PERIOD (SINCE 1868)

Towards the end of the Edo period Japan was forced to open its borders and enter into trading relationships with other nations. It was the American navy which first made Japan sign trade agreements in 1853. Shortly afterwards agreements were signed with Britain, Russia, France and the Netherlands. The Shogunate was removed in 1868 and the emperor returned to power. One result of this was that Buddhism and Shinto were separated. Buddhist images were taken out of Shinto shrines and Buddhist monks living at those shrines were disrobed. Followers of Shinto were made to have Shinto rather than Buddhist funerals.

### Growth of New Religions

Probably the most outstanding feature in the religious life of Japan since the Second World War has been the growth of the 'new religions'. Most of these are lay organisations and many of them concentrate on obtaining this-worldly benefits rather than on obtaining benefits after death such as rebirth in the Pure Land of Amida Buddha. The most successful of these new movements have been those associated with Nichiren Buddhism: the Nichiren Shoshu (the True Nichiren school) in particular. Two of these movements have a very large membership and great influence. They are the Rissho Koseikai and the Soka Gakkai.

*Rissho Koseikai*
The Rissho Koseikai offers a tolerant version of Nichiren Buddhism. The importance of the Lotus Sutra and Sakyamuni Buddha are stressed, but so too are personal development and skilful living in the world. Regular group discussion is one of the main features of this religion. Unlike its rival, the Soka Gakkai, it tries to keep religion and politics separate.

*Soka Gakkai*
Soka Gakkai is the largest of all the new religions in Japan. Its teachings are a mixture of Nichiren Shoshu and the ideas of its founder, Tsunesaburo Makiguchi (1871–1944). The title 'Soka Gakkai' means 'Learned Society for Value Creation'. It is taken from Makiguchi's belief that the three main values for society are the profitable (which expresses the value of all human life), the beautiful (the value of an individual) and the good (the value of the community). Representatives of the Soka Gakkai started to be elected to political office in 1955. Since then both their numbers and their political influence have grown considerably.

Despite its claim to be working towards world peace, Soka Gakkai has been criticised for its conversion technique called *shakubuku*, which literally means 'breaking and subduing'. This teaching developed from earlier Buddhist ideas that before a person could experience the true nature of things his or her false views had to be removed. The *shakubuku* technique works by a number of people questioning and challenging the potential convert's beliefs until he or she becomes exhausted, which is when the Soka Gakkai teachings are introduced.

In spite of the criticisms, Soka Gakkai is likely to remain a prominent feature of Japanese religious life and, through the Nichiren Shoshu sect, in many other countries as well.

## Traditional Japanese Buddhism Still Important

Although many of the traditional forms of Japanese Buddhism have declined in terms of numbers and influence during the modern period, they have become more able to change and adapt to the needs of modern people. A large number of young Japanese are turning to Zen Buddhism and the *do* traditions associated with it. As Japan modernises, many people want to keep traditional values, many of which come from Buddhist sources. Even though Japanese society has gone through great changes whilst adapting to the modern world, a view of life which is greatly influenced by Buddhism is likely to be around for some time to come.

1   How was Japanese Buddhism affected by the overthrow of the Shogunate in 1868?

2   **a** Name two of the 'new religions' which have become important in Japan since the Second World War.
    **b** With which school of Buddhism are they associated?

3   Name the conversion technique used by the largest of these 'new religions' and explain how it works.

4   In what ways can Buddhism be said to have benefited from the changes that have occurred in Japan since the Second World War?

# Chapter 18

# The Northern Route: The Himalayan Region

*The land of snows*

**TIBET**

Many people in Europe and America think of Tibet and its art as typically Buddhist. Tibet, the land of snows, and Buddhism are one and the same in the minds of many Westeners. Yet Buddhism was introduced into Tibet at a relatively late date. Although most of Tibet is located on the Himalayan plateau and extends along India's northern border (see the map on p. 58), Buddhism did not arrive there until the middle of the seventh century CE, over 1000 years after the death of the Buddha.

## Buddhism's Late Arrival in Tibet

Why did it take so long for Buddhism to reach Tibet? One reason is that until the seventh century Tibet was a divided land. The fertile valleys were ruled by various clans which were often at war with each other. Nomadic tribes lived on the vast plains of the central plateau. There was, therefore, little to attract Buddhist missionaries. Another reason is that the great trade routes between India, Central Asia and China all went around Tibet. Hence Japan, some 3000 miles from the Buddha's birthplace, received Buddhism before Tibet did.

Both because of, and in spite of, its late arrival, Buddhism enjoyed some advantages in Tibet. First of all, the Tibetans were able to take their Buddhism directly from India. Secondly, they were introduced to all three 'turnings of the wheel of *dharma*' (see p. 78) at more or less the same time. They were, therefore, able to make better sense of the various texts than the Chinese and Japanese, who acquired them rather haphazardly. Thirdly, since the Tibetans did not have such a sophisticated literary and religious culture of their own, they did not have the same problems of misunderstanding Buddhist ideas that the Chinese, for example, had.

## The Establishment of Buddhism in Tibet

There is some evidence that Buddhism was taken to Tibet during the reign of King

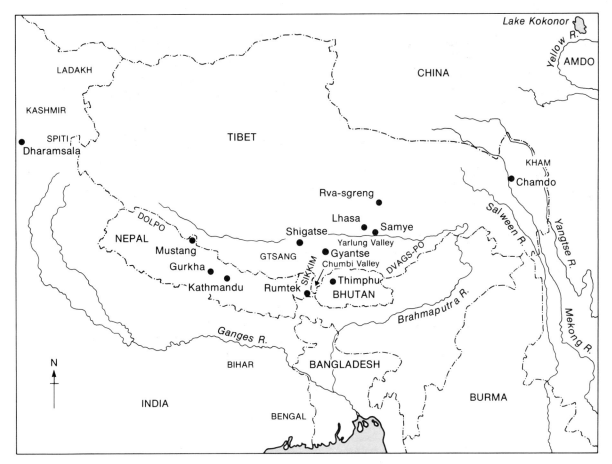

*Tibet*

Song-san-gam-po (died 650 CE), but Buddhism does not appear in official documents until the time of King Tri-song-de-tsen (740–98).

To help establish Buddhism, the king invited the Indian Buddhist teacher Santaraksita to Tibet. Santaraksita was a monk and a scholar. He decided that Tibet's first Buddhist monastery should be built at Samye, to the south-east of Lhasa, the capital. Unfortunately, bad omens plagued the building and opposition to the new religion increased to such an extent that Santaraksita had to leave the country. All was not lost for the Buddhists, however. A Tantric *siddha*, called Padma Sambhava, came to Tibet and defeated the 'demons' who were delaying the construction of the monastery. Padma Sambhava was able to supervise the completion of the building, which was opened some time around 779 CE. It was here that seven Tibetans received the first ordinations to be carried out on Tibetan soil.

From that time onwards Tibetan Buddhism developed a distinctive form of disciplined monastic life, incorporating study of the scriptures with various kinds of Tantric practice. This was reinforced by the teachings of a talented Buddhist monk who taught in Tibet during the early eleventh century CE. This was Atisa (982–1054). He was both a great scholar and a Tantric master.

1    When was Buddhism first introduced into Tibet?
2    Name three Indian Buddhist teachers who helped to establish Buddhism in Tibet.
3    Where was the first Tibetan Buddhist monastery built?
4    Imagine you are an Indian Buddhist who has been invited to Tibet to preach the Buddhist *Dharma*. Write a letter to a friend about the kinds of experiences you are having.

## The Schools of Tibetan Buddhism

The eleventh and twelfth centuries were very important for the development of Buddhism in Tibet. It was at this time that the four main schools of Tibetan Buddhism were established. All of these schools require their members to study and to meditate, though in different amounts.

### The Sakya school
This school was founded in 1073 by the Tibetan teacher Dromi (992–1074), who had studied for eight years in India. In the Sakya school there is a roughly equal emphasis placed on study and meditation. One of the most famous Sakya teachers was Chagpa (1235–80). He was especially liked by the Mongol emperor of China, Khublai Khan, because he defeated Taoist and Christian priests in a duel of magic. It was partly because of the respect won by Chagpa that the Mongols did not invade Tibet.

### The Kagyu school
This school was founded by Marpa (1012–96), who also studied in India. He was often called 'the translator' because he translated many Indian Buddhist texts into Tibetan. Marpa was also a great Tantric master whose own teacher, the Indian Tantric *siddha* Naropa, had given him lessons in six different kinds of Tantric meditation. Marpa's disciple Milarepa is one of Tibet's most famous and well-loved characters. After learning black magic in his youth and killing some relatives who

had robbed him of his inheritance, Milarepa became concerned about the consequences of such wicked acts. So he went to Marpa and asked to be taught the Tantric practices which would help him to escape from *samsara* in a single lifetime. Marpa made Milarepa perform many painful and difficult tasks before teaching him. Eventually he gave Milarepa the teaching he wanted, and Milarepa quickly became enlightened. Both men were expert meditators and today the Kagyu school, like its founders, puts greater emphasis on meditation than study.

### The Gelug school

This school was founded by Tsong Khapa (1357–1419). It was not, however, a new school in the way that the Sakya and Kagyu were. Rather, the Gelug school is a changed version of an earlier school, the Kadam, which was founded by Drom, a disciple of Atisa. The Kadam school taught the importance of monastic discipline and regulations more than the other schools did. Unlike the members of the other schools, Kadam monks were not allowed to marry or use intoxicants or money. Tsong Khapa studied in many different Tibetan monasteries before settling down with the Kadam school. He based most of his own teaching on the works of great Indian Buddhists such as Nagarjuna and Asanga. Eventually, his own branch of the Kadam school grew so big that it absorbed all the other branches into itself.

The Gelug school became the most powerful of all the Tibetan schools. Their head is the Dalai Lama, which means 'Ocean Teacher'. The Gelug school puts more emphasis on study than any of the other Tibetan Buddhist schools.

### The Nyingma school

The fourth Tibetan Buddhist school is called the Nyingma. Nyingma Buddhists trace their beginnings back to Padma Sambhava and base their practices on the Tantric texts he brought with him. They believed that Padma Sambhava, who is often called Guru Rinpoche (Precious Teacher), hid many Tantric texts, known as 'treasures', in various parts of Tibet. These would remain hidden until the time was right for them to be discovered. So instead of spending their time translating Buddhist texts from Sanskrit and other Indian languages, the followers of the Nyingma school looked for and discovered many 'treasures'. However, many of these 'treasures' were not accepted as true scriptures by the other schools. This, along with the fact that the Nyingma members were organised in a much looser way than in other schools, has tended to make the Nyingma school quite distinctive.

**?**

1   Link the teacher with the appropriate school:
    Marpa              Gelug
    Chagpa             Nyingma
    Tsong Khapa        Kagyu
    Guru Rinpoche      Sakya
2   Which of the teachers listed above was Milarepa's spiritual master?
3   Which Tibetan Buddhist school puts most emphasis on study?
4   Name the school which has the Dalai Lama as its head.
5   Which Tibetan Buddhist school places most emphasis on finding 'treasure' texts?

From the late fourteenth century onwards the main events and changes in Tibetan Buddhism were:

- the completion of translations and the putting together of the Tibetan Buddhist Canon of scripture;

- the growth of the doctrine of reincarnating *lamas*.

## The Tibetan Buddhist Canon

The scriptures of the Tibetan Buddhists are divided into two main parts:

- **the Kanjur**, which is composed of all texts (including the regulations for monks), both Hinayana and Mahayana, attributed to the Buddha;

- **the Tenjur**, the textbooks and commentaries which arrange the Buddha's teaching in terms of themes or offer explanations of various parts of Buddhist teaching.

The Kanjur consists of 108 volumes, the Tenjur 225 volumes.

## Reincarnating *Lamas*

There were already legends in Tibet about some of the early kings being incarnations of heavenly *bodhisattvas*. The Sakya school applied this idea to some of the most saintly of their own *lamas*, who came to be thought of as incarnations of earlier holy teachers. Soon other schools were able to pick out some of their own holy men as reincarnations of great teachers from the past. In time the Dalai Lama came to be seen as the reincarnation of the Dalai Lama before him and, at the same time, an incarnation of the *bodhisattva* Avalokitesvara (Chen Rezi in Tibetan) (see pp. 70–1).

1   Name the Tibetan Buddhist collection of scriptures which contains the teachings of the Buddha.
2   Name the Tibetan Buddhist collection of scriptures which contains the textbooks by later Buddhists.
3   How many volumes make up each of these collections?
4   The Dalai Lama is believed to be an incarnation of the previous Dalai Lama and which *bodhisattva*?

## The Situation in Tibet Today

Buddhism has suffered more than any other religion from the spread of communism in Asia. In 1950 the Chinese army entered Tibet and took over the country. The Tibetans, however, rebelled against the many cruel and degrading practices of the Chinese. Monks were killed or disrobed, nuns were either married to Chinese soldiers or made pregnant by them. Buddhist images were smashed and stones with sacred carvings on them were used for paving the ground in toilets. In 1959 the Tibetans rebelled again but, as in 1950, they were defeated.

After the 1959 uprising the Dalai Lama and many other Tibetans, most of them highly trained and experienced monks, had to flee the country. The Dalai Lama, through the generosity of the Indian government, was able to take up residence at Dharamsala in northern India. Other monks went to different parts of India. Still others moved to Europe or the United States and set up monasteries or study centres. At the present time Tibetan Buddhism looks more likely to survive outside Tibet than in the land of snows itself.

**?**

1    In what year did Communist China's army first enter Tibet?
2    How did the Chinese treat the Tibetans after the invasion?
3    In which two years did the Tibetans rise up against the Chinese?
4    Where does the Dalai Lama live now?
5    Find out all you can about the Dalai Lama's peaceful attempts to free Tibet.

**NEPAL**    Many people think that the Buddha was born in Nepal. It is true that the Lumbini Grove where he entered the world is now within the borders of Nepal, but at the time of the Buddha those borders were much further to the north. The available evidence suggests that Buddhism was taken to the Kathmandu valley (the heartland of Nepal) around the time of Asoka. Buddhism was not, however, the only religion to be taken from India to Nepal. What we now call Hinduism also has a long history in Nepal.

## The People of Nepal: the Newars and the Gurkhas

Two main races of people live in Nepal. The oldest inhabitants are the Newars, who live mainly in the eastern part of the country. They are mostly Buddhist. The other race is that of the Gurkhas. These people moved into Nepal around the time of the Muslim invasions of India. They live mainly in the western part of the country. Their religion is mostly Hindu.

## Nepalese Buddhism

The kind of Buddhism practised by the Nepalese is mainly Tantric, though it is clear that it has also been influenced by Hinduism. The Nepalese Buddhist community is divided into groups which are similar to the castes of Hinduism. The monks have married and turned into professional priests. Sons have followed their fathers in this occupation and it has become hereditary. Now, only sons from 'priestly' families can become priests.

There are two types of Buddhist monk-priests in Nepal: the monk (*bhiksu*) and the diamond teacher (*vajra acarya*). The monks have passed through a basic ordination or initiation ritual, the diamond teachers have been initiated into Tantric practices as well. These they pass on to chosen disciples. Both groups perform rituals for members of the community, as well as taking a leading role at festivals and performing merit-making activities such as reading from the Buddhist scriptures.

In the modern period, both Theravada and Tibetan Buddhists have settled in

Nepal. As yet, they do not seem to have had much success in converting the Nepalese Buddhists to their versions of the religion.

1    Name the two main religions found in Nepal.
2    Name the two main races living in Nepal.
3    What kind of Buddhism is practised by the Nepalese?
4    In what ways has Nepalese Buddhism been affected by Hinduism?

**BHUTAN**    During the sixteenth century, Tibetan Buddhism spread to a number of small Himalayan countries. The most important were Ladakh in the west and Sikkhim and Bhutan in the east. The first two are now part of India, but Bhutan has remained independent. It is the only Asian country where Mahayana Buddhism is the official religion. The Bhutanese have had to fight for their freedom on more than one occasion, as indicated by the Bhutanese word for monastery, which is *zong*, meaning 'fort'. It is the Kagyu form of Tibetan Buddhism which has been most important for the development of Buddhism in Bhutan. Unlike their Tibetan fellows, the Kagyu monks of Bhutan are usually celibate.

The king of Bhutan wants to keep traditional Buddhism alive in his country and so follows a policy of restricting the number of tourists who visit it each year. How long such a policy will protect the traditional Bhutanese lifestyle from destruction through contact with Western civilisation is not certain. One thing is clear though – the Bhutanese will not give in without a struggle.

1    What is the official religion of Bhutan?
2    What is the Bhutanese name for monastery and what does it tell us about the history of Bhutan?
3    Why might Western civilisation be a threat to the Bhutanese way of life? Discuss your answers.

## Chapter 19

# *Buddhism in Europe and the USA*

Buddhism came to Europe and North America by two more or less independent routes. One of these was through scholarly books about Buddhism and translations of Buddhist scriptures. The other was through Buddhists coming to live in the West and Westerners becoming practising Buddhists.

**DISCOVERING BUDDHISM FROM BOOKS**

Two of the more famous early scholars who wrote about Buddhism and translated Buddhist texts are the German philosopher Arthur Schopenhauer and his countryman Hermann Oldenberg. Oldenberg edited the Vinaya Pitaka of the Pali Canon and wrote one of the first scholarly books about the Buddha. In France, Eugene Burnouf translated the Lotus Sutra into French and wrote a history of Indian Buddhism. In Britain, the main figures were Sir Edwin Arnold, whose poem *The Light of Asia* brought many English-speaking people into contact with Buddhist ideas for the first time, and Thomas William Rhys Davids. This energetic Welshman founded the Pali Text Society (which is dedicated to publishing editions and translations of Buddhist scriptures), translated the Digha Nikaya (a part of the Sutta Pitaka) and wrote many articles about Buddhism. In the USA, Henry Clarke Warren translated many Theravada texts into English whilst the Russian Theodore Stcherbatsky worked with late Mahayana texts.

**DISCOVERING BUDDHISM FROM IMMIGRANTS**

The main group of Buddhist immigrants to the USA were from China and Japan. They went first to Hawaii and then to the west coast, California in particular. Most of these immigrants were followers of the True Pure Land Teaching (Jodo Shinshu) (see p. 109). In the twentieth century they have organised themselves into the Buddhist Churches of America. To a certain extent this title reflects the way that Japanese American Buddhists have changed their services and organisation to fit the American situation. Another reason for using the title 'church', however, is that 'churches' can register as charities and avoid paying taxes.

**BUDDHISM IN THE USA**

Many Americans have become Buddhists, especially since the Second World War. A fair number of these have joined Zen Buddhist groups which were set up by Japanese Zen masters. Theravada and Tibetan Buddhism have also attracted followers. The total number of Buddhists in contemporary America is well below one million, however.

**BUDDHISM IN BRITAIN**

In Britain, the tradition of living Buddhism goes back to an Englishman named Allan Bennett. In 1890, when he was 18 years old, Bennett read Sir Edwin Arnold's *The Light of Asia*. He became so attracted to Buddhism that soon afterwards he went to

Sri Lanka and then on to Burma where he was ordained under the name Ananda Maitreya. He later changed this into its Pali form of Ananda Metteyya. However, not until 1926, when Anagarika Dharmapala (a Sinhalese Buddhist) founded the British Maha Bodhi Society (Society of the Great Awakening), did Buddhism really become a religious option for British people.

Since then, Theravada Buddhism has proved to be the most popular form of Buddhism among the British. Tibetan Buddhism has also attracted a considerable number of followers. Zen has not become as popular as in the USA, though another Japanese movement, Nichiren Shoshu, is attracting an increasing number of British people.

## The Western Buddhist Order

Perhaps most distinctive of all Buddhist groups in Britain is the Western Buddhist Order (WBO) and its wider organisation, Friends of the Western Buddhist Order (FWBO). The FWBO was founded in 1967 by an Englishman called Dennis Lingwood, who was ordained under the name of Sangharakshita, which means 'Protector of the Community'. Lingwood studied under teachers from Zen, Theravada and Tibetan traditions and he came to the conclusion that just as Buddhism had changed when it was taken outside India, so it would change when introduced into Western society. His Western Buddhist Order is his attempt to make Buddhism workable in the West. (See p. 135 for some important events in the FWBO year.)

**?**

1   What were the two ways by which Buddhism came to the West?
2   Name two Britons who made Buddhist teachings available to English-speaking people.
3   Which Buddhist group is the main representative of Buddhism in Britain?
4   Name the founder of the Maha Bodhi Society.
5   Write a letter to a friend explaining the main differences between Buddhism in the USA and Buddhism in Britain.
6   Try to find out why Buddhism attracts some Britons. See if you can discuss this with a local Buddhist group.

<table>
<tr><td>

**Chapter**

**20**

</td><td>

# *Buddhism in Modern India*

</td></tr>
</table>

Now we come full circle and return to the birthplace of Buddhism. Although absent for many years, Buddhism is now making a comeback in India. There are three channels for this: the Maha Bodhi Society, ex-untouchable Buddhist groups, and Tibetan Buddhists.

## THE MAHA BODHI SOCIETY IN INDIA

The main focus of the Maha Bodhi Society's efforts in India was the reclaiming of Buddhist sites from the Hindu priests who had taken control of them. In this they were very successful. The modern visitor to India can visit many Buddhist holy places and find them looked after by Buddhists. However, the Maha Bodhi Society made few converts. In the words of one Indian Buddhist, the Maha Bodhi Society 'cared more for stones than for men'.

## EX-UNTOUCHABLE BUDDHIST GROUPS

The second channel was opened up by Dr B.R. Ambedkar, a leader of the lowest group in Hindu society, the untouchables. After India obtained independence from British rule in 1947, Ambedkar decided that the untouchables would get a better deal and be more able to improve their self-esteem if they became Buddhists. In 1956 he publicly converted to Buddhism and many untouchables followed him. Although he died that same year, Ambedkar left an organisation which was able to hold the newly converted Buddhists together. There are now around four million Buddhists in India who are connected with the movement begun by Ambedkar.

## TIBETAN BUDDHISTS IN INDIA

The third channel came into being as a result of the Chinese invasion of Tibet in 1959. Many Tibetans left the country of their birth and settled in India. These exiles come from a variety of Tibetan Buddhist sub-groups and from different parts of Tibet. Many monks, both young and old, are studying and training at the various Maha Bodhi centres across the country, others have set up their own centres. Some Tibetan Buddhists have made contact with members of the Buddhist movement founded by Dr Ambedkar. Although there have been difficulties, one of the main ones being the fact that they speak different languages, this association is likely to be of benefit to both groups.

Buddhism is back in India but, as yet, it is not firmly re-established in the land of its birth. India is a rapidly changing country but the Buddha was one of her greatest men. His influence has affected the entire culture. So here, if anywhere, Buddhism should be able to feel at home.

**?**

1 What was the main concern of the Maha Bodhi Society in its early days?
2 In what ways did the efforts of the Maha Bodhi Society contribute to the reintroduction of Buddhism in India?
3 Name the leader of the untouchables who encouraged them to convert to Buddhism.

| Chapter 21 | *Theravada Festivals and Ceremonies* |

Most people the world over have special times when they remember things which happened in the past or when they look forward to the future. Birthdays, Remembrance Sunday and New Year's Day are some familiar examples.

Buddhist festivals and ceremonies are special times when Buddhists look back to the past or forward to the future. Most important Buddhist celebrations and festivals are held at the time of the full moon. Not only is this a special time, the main events in the Buddha's life are said to have happened at full moon time. It is also the part of each month when nights are lightest.

Remember that when Buddhism spread from India it moved eastwards by two main routes: a southern route by way of south-east Asian countries and a northern route by way of Central Asia, China, Korea, Japan and the Himalayan countries. When we look at Buddhist festivals and ceremonies, we see that there is often quite a difference between those of the southern route and those of the northern route. So we will deal with each separately.

The main kind of Buddhism that we find in the southern route countries is Theravada (the Way of the Elders). Theravada Buddhists have certain festivals and ceremonies in common and some which are unique to a particular country. In this chapter we will look at three events which are celebrated by most Theravada Buddhists.

## VAISAKHA (WESAK)

Vaisakha or Wesak is probably the most important Theravada Buddhist festival. It is celebrated at the full moon in May or June and focuses on the birth, enlightenment and death of the Buddha. Buddhists remember these events with happiness because they are reminded of how lucky they are to have come across the Buddha's teachings.

In many Theravada countries, for example Sri Lanka and Thailand, lights are important symbols at this festival as they remind Buddhists of the Buddha's enlightenment. In Burma, watering the bodhi tree is a popular practice at this time. The lay people usually make offerings to the monks at Wesak. This helps them to earn merit and keep them in contact with the local monastery. In some Theravada countries, such as Thailand, monks and lay people often walk around the monastery three times carrying lighted candles on Wesak night. This is a kind of taking refuge: the first time round they think of the Buddha, the second time they think of the *Dharma* and the third time they think of the *Sangha*. Sometimes people

*The Wesak festival*

in Buddhist countries go on a pilgrimage to holy places at Wesak time and they often send cards to each other.

**?**

1   What three events are celebrated at the Wesak festival?
2   What do Buddhists remember each time they walk around the monastery at Wesak time?
3   Why do you think the Wesak festival is a happy time for Theravada Buddhists?
4   Festivals unite communities. How does Wesak do this?

## KATHINA

During the tropical rainy season (beginning at the full moon in July or August), Buddhist monks and nuns often go into retreat. They spend much of this time in meditation or study – 'recharging their batteries' – and do not usually have much contact with the lay people.

The Kathina festival takes place at the end of the rainy season which, in India and nearby countries, is in October or November. For Buddhists this is a very happy time. The lay people usually go to the monastery to greet the monks and congratulate them on the completion of the retreat. They bring all kinds of presents and turn the event into a great celebration. In Theravada Buddhist countries it is believed that all the people, rich and poor alike, share in the merit gained by providing the monks with all they need for their simple lifestyle. Often, those who have given their presents, and those who are too poor to provide one, stand by the path along which the present-givers walk. Then they touch the presents as they go past. This, they believe, makes sure they get a share of the merit.

*A Kathina ceremony*

## A Robe-Giving Ceremony

The most important activity that takes place at this festival is the Kathina ceremony itself. Kathina is a robe-giving ceremony. The lay people give the cloth for a robe, which the monks then have to make into a finished garment within a single day. The design of the robe is based on the layout of the paddy fields in the kingdom of Magadha at the time of the Buddha. One monk is chosen to receive the robe at the ceremony. Sometimes this is the monk who has been ordained longest, sometimes it is a monk chosen by the abbot. Only one Kathina robe can be offered to a monastery in any one year. The Kathina ceremony marks the return of the monks to their normal routine; the gift of a new robe symbolises a new start and gives a sense of beginning afresh.

**?**

1   At what time of year is the Kathina festival held?
2   How do the people in Theravada Buddhist countries make sure that everyone shares in the merit that comes from giving presents to the monks?
3   **a** What does the giving of a new robe symbolise?
    **b** What kinds of new resolutions might a monk make at this time?
4   On what pattern is the design of the new robe based?
5   Why do you think the lay people are required to provide just the cloth rather than the finished garment?
6   What effect might ceremonies like Kathina have on the relationship between monks and lay people?

**PARITTA (PIRIT)**

The Paritta ceremony (sometimes called Pirit) is a ceremony of protection. The word comes from the Sanskrit *paritra* meaning 'safety'. Unlike Wesak and Kathina, which are annual events, Paritta ceremonies can take place as often as people want. In fact, most celebrations of any significance, whether domestic, village or national, include a Paritta.

## Chanting from Scriptures

The main part of the Paritta is the chanting of selected Buddhist scriptures (*suttas*) from the Pali Canon. Most well used are the Mangala Sutta, which sets out the activities by which people can obtain blessings or spiritual benefits; the Ratana Sutta, which was spoken by the Buddha to cure the people of Vaisali; and the Karaniya Metta Sutta, which encourages monks to practise lovingkindness (*metta*). These three *suttas* are so popular that they have been reproduced on record and cassette in some Theravada countries, and most children know at least some of them off by heart. The actual *suttas* chosen for reciting at the Paritta ceremony will be worked out according to the reason the ceremony is being held. Different texts would be used for protecting a new building and for curing sickness, for example.

*A Pirit ceremony*

### The Ceremony

Paritta ceremonies can be quite short, an hour or so, or they can last for several days. At the shorter forms of the ceremony there has to be an odd number of monks (three or more). At the longer ceremonies the number has to be even. The longer ceremonies are much more elaborate. They start with the taking of refuge in the *Buddha*, the *Dharma* and the *Sangha* and with the recitation of the five precepts and other important Buddhist teachings. (The five precepts are non-injury, not stealing, not lying, chastity and temperance.) A relic of the Buddha is usually present. This, along with the *suttas* to be chanted and the monks, symbolises the Triple Gem (*Buddha*, *Dharma*, *Sangha*). A thread connects the chairs on which the monks sit and pots of water are placed around the site, which often has a special cloth hung over it. At the end of the ceremony the thread is divided and tied around the wrists and necks of the people, who are also sprinkled with water from the pots. This makes sure that the blessings from the ceremony are taken away by all those who were present.

1  What does the word *paritra* mean?
2  What is the main part of the Paritta ceremony?
3  Name the three most popular *suttas* for Paritta ceremonies.
4  In what way are the three jewels (Triple Gem) present at Paritta ceremonies?
5  How might chanting Pali texts act as a kind of protection and blessing for Buddhists? Discuss your answers.

| Chapter 22 | *Mahayana Festivals and Ceremonies* |
|---|---|

The most influential form of Buddhism in the countries on the northern route is the Mahayana. As we saw in Chapter 11 and in Chapters 16–18, Mahayana Buddhism is made up of many schools. It also recognises a wide variety of scriptures and is good at changing to fit in with local conditions. All of these points can make a description of northern route Buddhism quite complicated. So in this chapter we will look at just a few examples of Mahayana festivals, two from Japanese Buddhism and two from Tibetan Buddhism.

## JAPANESE BUDDHIST FESTIVALS

Both festivals in this section show how Buddhism can adapt to local circumstances. The first, O-bon, shows how Buddhism is able to fit in with Chinese and Japanese ideas about honouring ancestors; the second, Hana Matsuri, is a good example of Buddhism fitting in with people's feelings about celebrating the changes in the seasons.

### O-bon

The O-bon festival is held every year, usually from 13 July to 15 July. Family ancestors are the main focus of this festival. Although O-bon is not a public holiday, many Japanese take a day or two off work to return to their home towns.

*Welcoming the ancestors*
On the first day the ancestors are invited into the home with a welcoming fire and often with candles, flowers and food as well. In some places a bonfire is lit on a nearby hillside as a communal welcome. In many ways the festival acts as a family reunion and reminds people about the importance of their family. The second day is the main part of the festival. The most popular form of celebration is a kind of fete where all the people from the locality get together for dancing. The musicians set up on a type of bandstand, which is often specially erected for the purpose, and the people dance around it. Games are played and everyone eats party food. All in all, a sense of connectedness with one's family ancestors and one's neighbours (including their ancestors) is created. On the final day the family's ancestors are waved off with the lighting of a farewell fire and the offering of fruit and flowers to the Buddha, along with a request for blessings on the family and its ancestors.

*A visit from a Buddhist monk*
O-bon is one of the busiest times of year for the Buddhist monks. The monks try to visit as many families as possible during the three days of the festival. In a simple ceremony before the household shrine the monk recites selected passages from the Buddhist scriptures. A favourite story at this festival is one about how the Buddha's disciple Maudgalyayana rescued his departed mother from Hell.

**1**   In what way are the ancestors welcomed at the beginning of the O-bon festival?
**2**   What kinds of activities take place on the second day of the festival?
**3**   What part do Buddhist monks play in O-bon?
**4**   How does this festival show the ways in which Buddhism adapts to local conditions?
**5**   How does the Japanese belief that the spirits of the ancestors return home each year for the O-bon festival fit with the Buddhist teaching about rebirth? Discuss your answers.

## Hana Matsuri

*Preparing for the Hana Matsuri festival*

Hana Matsuri, the flower festival, is held every spring on 8 April. At this time of year the cherry blossom, for which Japan is famous all over the world, is in flower. Spring is the time of new life. Not surprisingly, this festival celebrates the birth of the Buddha. Look back to Chapter 6 to remind yourself of the story of his birth.

In many Japanese monasteries a large model of a white elephant (a symbol of the *bodhisattva*) is set up in the courtyard on Hana Matsuri day. The people make flower displays which represent the Lumbini Grove in which Queen Maya and her child can be seen. A favourite activity for many children is pouring delicately scented tea over the image of the baby. This simple ritual reminds them of how the gods poured two streams of water from the sky to wash the newly born infant. Hana Matsuri is a happy festival and stalls selling food and goods are set up in the monastery courtyard. Dancing and acrobatics are also popular activities during this festival.

| ? | 1 | What event is celebrated at the Hana Matsuri festival? |
|---|---|---|
| | 2 | Why do you think this festival is celebrated when the cherry blossom is in flower? |
| | 3 | What does the white elephant symbolise? |
| | 4 | Explain the symbolic aspects of the story of the Buddha's birth, for example the baby walking and talking, streams of water flowing from the sky. |

## TIBETAN BUDDHIST FESTIVALS AND CEREMONIES

The great celebrations and festivals of Tibetan Buddhism are no longer carried out on the grand scale that could be seen before the Chinese invasion in 1950. In Tibet, the Chinese army of occupation stops the local people from celebrating in the traditional way. Outside Tibet, wherever there is a Tibetan community of any size, the main festivals are still celebrated, although on a smaller scale. This is also true of communities where Western converts to Tibetan Buddhism follow a Tibetan teacher (*lama*). Here, however, not all parts of Tibetan culture are present.

The first of the two Tibetan Buddhist festivals described below is firmly rooted in Tibetan culture and is most celebrated by Tibetan exiles. The second is more strictly Buddhist, a festival that Western followers of Tibetan Buddhism can identify with.

### Losar, the New Year Festival

*Butter sculptures*

For the Tibetans, the new year begins at the time of the new moon in February. The celebrations last for 15 days, until the full moon has arrived. Losar is the longest lasting festival in the whole of the Tibetan Buddhist calendar.

### A new start and scaring away evil spirits

As in the West, New Year is a time for leaving behind old habits and cultivating new ones. Tibetan Buddhists also use this time to do their spring cleaning. Houses are thoroughly cleaned and clothes washed. In addition, evil spirits which might have settled in amongst the community during the previous year are scared away with special spirit-frightening ceremonies. The monks dress up in colourful clothes and perform traditional rituals, whilst the lay people light torches and firecrackers and run through their homes shouting and yelling. These combined efforts make sure that no evil spirits are left behind to bother people in the new year.

Once the cleaning and spirit frightening has been completed, the people decorate their homes. Then the celebrations begin. Family shrines are attended to and special food is cooked. Many Tibetan families will take the opportunity to visit their friends and neighbours at this time. This makes sure that the special food is shared around and that everyone benefits – including poor people, who are given gifts at New Year.

### Butter sculptures and puppet shows

Traditionally, an important part of the Losar celebrations was the butter sculpture contest. The February climate in Tibet is too cold for butter to melt naturally. It therefore offers an extremely fine medium for sculpture. Over the years the monks have become very skilful in this art form. This skill can still be seen in Tibetan Buddhist monasteries in the Himalayan areas around Tibet. Prizes were awarded for the best sculptures and monasteries acquired reputations for their high quality work. Puppet shows were also very popular and still are in those areas where Tibetan exiles have settled. The puppeteers will often base their performances on traditional Tibetan tales and stories taken from the Buddhist scriptures. This helps to keep both the culture and the religion alive for the people.

1   What is the name of the Tibetan New Year festival?
2   How do the Tibetans frighten away evil spirits at the end of the old year?
3   List some of the ways in which ordinary Tibetans celebrate New Year.
4   Name two activities likely to take place in a traditional Tibetan Buddhist monastery at New Year.
5   Write a letter to a friend comparing the Tibetan New Year festival with any other New Year festival you are familiar with. Pay special attention to the similarities and differences between the two.

## Guru Rinpoche's Birthday

Guru Rinpoche (Precious Teacher) is a name given by Tibetan Buddhists to Padma Sambhava, the Indian Tantric teacher who helped establish Buddhism in Tibet during the eighth century CE. Although Padma Sambhava is linked with the Nyingma school of Buddhism, he is referred to by all Tibetan Buddhists as Guru Rinpoche. His birthday is celebrated during the summer month of July. It is a time for gladness and joy, and also a time for meditation.

*Guru Rinpoche*

Padma Sambhava was a great meditator and it is for his teachings about Tantric meditations (as well as his great magical powers) that he is best remembered. So, in the West, the celebration of Padma Sambhava's birthday focuses mainly on the meditation.

## The ceremony

Often, the local Tibetan Buddhist centre will hold a ceremony on the day of the festival. It is usually held in the shrine room, which is richly decorated for the occasion. Incense is burned, many candles and night lights are lit, beautiful carpets are laid on the floor and flowers are placed all around the room. The atmosphere is very quiet and peaceful.

The ceremony begins with the offering of food and light to the Buddha. This is a Buddhist way of offering up desires, desires that prevent the mind from awakening to the truth. Then the chanting meditation begins. It is difficult to describe the feeling of being in a room where Tibetan Buddhists are chanting, but for many people it is a very powerful experience. After the chanting comes visualisation meditation, for which the mind needs to be very calm and concentrated. By practising visualisation, Tibetan Buddhists try to improve their compassion and wisdom. This helps them to put the Buddha's teachings into practice.

Like most festivals, Guru Rinpoche's birthday includes a party. After the meditation, the Tibetan Buddhists usually gather together to eat the food that has been offered and to have a bit of fun – dancing, for example, or telling stories.

**?**

1    What does the title Guru Rinpoche mean?
2    What was Guru Rinpoche's real name?
3    At what time of year is his birthday celebrated?
4    Name the two types of meditation practised during the ceremony.
5    Can you think why Tibetan Buddhists might want to spend most of the time at this festival meditating? Discuss your answers.

## A Daily Ritual

Symbols are important in all Tibetan Buddhist rituals. When preparing for daily meditation and worship, a Tibetan Buddhist will go to a shrine room if he or she is in a monastery or sit before a small shrine at home. Usually the shrine will have eight items on it:

- a pot of water;
- a second pot of water;
- flowers;
- incense;

- perfume;
- a light;
- some food;
- a shell.

Each of these is a symbol. The first pot of water symbolises the sense of touch and the quality of honouring the Buddha, for it is there to wash his feet. The second pot of water is a symbol of offering. It is there for the Buddha to drink. The flowers symbolise beauty and the sense of sight. The incense symbolises the sense of smell, so too does the perfume. The light is a symbol of understanding, food a symbol for the sense of taste. Finally, the shell represents sound and the sense of hearing.

Every time a Tibetan Buddhist worships at a shrine, the eight offerings are either changed or relit. The ritual as a whole symbolises the offering of all five senses and one's mind to the Buddha. Once a person has done this with sincerity, they are ready to begin their meditations.

**?**

1    Link the following items with what they symbolise:

| water | hearing |
| flowers | taste |
| perfume | sight |
| light | smell |
| food | understanding |
| shell | touch |

2    Why do you think a shell is chosen to represent sound?
3    Why do you think a meditator might want to offer all his or her senses to the Buddha before beginning to meditate? Discuss your answers.
4    What is a symbol? Observe a flower over a period of two to three weeks. What message might it give to a Buddhist?

# Chapter 23

# Buddhist Festivals Through the Year

**?**  Find out as much as you can about the Buddhist festivals celebrated in Britain that are listed on this calendar.

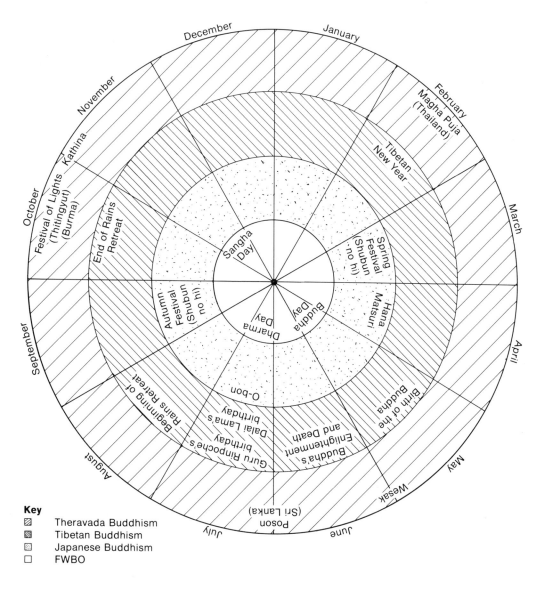

**Key**
- ▨ Theravada Buddhism
- ▩ Tibetan Buddhism
- ▩ Japanese Buddhism
- ☐ FWBO

# *Looking Back*

This book has not been written for Buddhists, though we hope some of them will find it interesting and enjoyable to read. It has been written for people who have an interest in Buddhism and want to know a little more about it. Parts of the book will have been interesting, parts of it will have been difficult. Now that you have come to the end and you look back, we hope that the material you have studied will be a little clearer in your mind.

We hope too that now, looking back, you have some idea of what it might be like to walk for a while in the shoes of a Buddhist and that you have found those shoes fairly comfortable. Whether you go off and get some for yourself is a decision we happily leave for you to make.

*Peter and Holly Connolly, 1991*

# *Further Reading and Resources*

**PUPILS' BOOKS**

A simple introduction to basic Buddhist teachings and practices is:
Peter and Holly Connolly, *Religions Through Festivals: Buddhism* (Longman, 1989).

**TEACHERS' BOOKS**

For the teacher, a recent and useful introduction is:
P. Harvey, *An Introduction to Buddhism* (Cambridge University Press, 1990).
*The World of Buddhism* edited by H. Bechert and R. Gombrich (Thames and Hudson, 1984) is also useful and contains many superb photographs.
Both of the above works contain useful bibliographies to guide further reading.

**SOME USEFUL ADDRESSES**

Tharpa Publications, 15 Bendemeer Road, London SW15 1JX. Publishers of books, pictures and videos on a variety of Buddhist topics.

Wisdom Publications, 402 Hoe Street, Walthamstow, E17 9AA. A Buddhist publisher of books and pictures. The editor has had considerable experience of working with teachers and is usually pleased to help out with enquiries from schools.

Tantra Designs, Gas Ferry Road, Bristol BS1 6UN. Publishers of Buddhist pictures and statuettes.

The Buddhist Society, 58 Eccleston Square, London SW1V 1PH. They sell a wide range of books on Buddhism and related subjects, run lectures and meditation classes and publish a regularly updated directory of Buddhist groups and centres in Britain.

Be adventurous, write to all of the above to find out what they offer. If you obtain a copy of the *Buddhist Directory* write to your nearest centres (include a stamped addressed envelope) asking how they feel about sending speakers to schools or receiving groups from schools.

# *Glossary*

**Abhidharma Piṭaka**  basket of higher teachings
**Ambedkar, B.R.**  Indian 'untouchable' leader who encouraged many of his followers to convert to Buddhism
**Amitābha (Amida)**  the Buddha of infinite light, creator of the Pure Land
**Ānanda**  the Buddha's attendant for the last 20 years of his life
*anātman*  no-self
*anitya*  impermanence
**Arada Kalāma**  one of the Buddha's meditation teachers
*arhat*  'worthy one', someone who became enlightened after putting the Buddha's teachings into practice
**Asanga**  founder of the Yogācāra school
**Asīta**  a hermit who made a prediction about Siddhārtha's future
**Aśoka**  emperor of India (ruled 269–232 BCE)
**Atisā**  (982–1054), an influential Buddhist missionary to Tibet
*ātman*  self
**Avalokiteśvara**  *bodhisattva* of compassion

**Bennett, Allan**  first Englishman to be ordained as a Buddhist monk, taking the name of Ānanda Maitreya (Ānanda Metteyya)
*bhikṣu*  monk
**Bhutan**  only country in the world to have Mahāyāna Buddhism as the official religion
*bodhisattva*  awakening being
**Brahma Vīhāra**  sublime state

**Ch'an**  the Meditation school, Chinese Mahāyāna
**Chen Rezi**  Tibetan name for Avalokiteśvara
**Ching-t'u**  Chinese Pure Land school
**Confucius (K'ung Fu-tzu)**  a famous Chinese philosopher
**Cunda**  the man who provided the Buddha's last meal

**Dalai Lama**  'Ocean Teacher', head of the Gelug school of Tibetan Buddhism and leader of the Tibetan people
*Dharma*  the Buddha's teachings
*dharma kāya*  truth body of the Buddha
**Dromi**  (992–1074), founder of the Śakya school of Tibetan Buddhism
*duḥkha*  unsatisfactoriness

*gandharva*  action-energy looking for a body
*guru*  Sanskrit word for teacher

**Hana Matsuri**  Japanese spring festival celebrating the birth of the Buddha
*hijiri*  wandering Japanese Buddhist preachers

**Hīnayāna**  Mahāyānists' name for non-Mahāyāna Buddhists
**Hōnen**  (1133–1212), founder of the Japanese Jōdo Shū (Pure Land) school
**Hua-yen**  Flower Garland school – a Chinese Mahāyāna school

**Jātaka**  stories of the Buddha's former lives

*kāma*  sexual desire
*kami*  native Japanese gods
**Kanjur**  Tibetan Buddhist scriptures attributed to the Buddha
*karma*  action
*karma vipāka*  action-energy
*karuṇā*  compassion
**Kaṭhina**  Theravāda robe-giving ceremony
*koan*  a kind of riddle designed to help a meditator become enlightened
**Kūkai**  (774–835), founder of the Japanese Shingon (True Word) school

*lama*  Tibetan word for teacher
**Lao Tzu**  a famous Chinese philosopher
**Losar**  Tibetan New Year festival
**Lotus Sūtra**  a Mahāyāna scripture

**Mādhyamaka**  the Middle Position, a philosophical school of Mahāyāna Buddhism
**Mahāprajāpati**  the Buddha's stepmother, sometimes said to be the first Buddhist nun
**Mahāsanghika**  the Great Community, an early school of Buddhism
**Mahāyāna**  the Great Vehicle, a form of Buddhism
**Mahendra (Mahinda)**  son of Aśoka, first Buddhist missionary to Sri Lanka
**Maitreya**  a *bodhisattva*, the future Buddha
**Manjuśri**  *bodhisattva* of insight or wisdom
*mantra*  a chant or 'mind shelter'
**Mantrayāna/Tantrayāna/Vajrayāna**  names for the third major development of Buddhism
**Mappo**  the period of spiritual decline
**Māra**  'the tempter', who tried to prevent Siddhārtha from becoming enlightened
**Marpa**  (1012–96), founder of the Kagyu school of Tibetan Buddhism
**Māyā**  the Buddha's mother
**Menandros (Milinda)**  king of north-western India, famous for his dialogue with the Buddhist monk Nāgasena
**Milarepa**  Marpa's most famous pupil

**Nāgārjuna**  founder of the Mādhyamaka school
**Naropa**  an Indian Tantric *siddha*
**Nichiren**  (1222–82 CE), founder of the Japanese Nichiren Shū (Nichiren school)

**nikāya**   *either* a tradition of ordination *or* a section of the Sūtra Piṭaka
**nirodha**   cessation, removal (of suffering)
**nirvāṇa**   extinction, the cessation of ignorance and suffering

**Obaku**   a Japanese version of the Meditation school (Zen) which was influenced by Pure Land teachings
**O-bon**   Japanese festival for ancestors

**Padma Sambhava (Guru Rinpoche)**   an Indian Tantric *siddha* who supervised the completion of the Samye monastery in Tibet; founder of the Nyingma school
**Pāli Canon**   scriptures of the Theravāda Buddhists
**Paritta (Pirit)**   a blessing ceremony
**Perfection of Wisdom Sūtras**   Mahāyāna scriptures
**prajñā**   insight or wisdom
**pratītya samutpāda**   dependent origination
**Pure Land**   a happy place created by the Buddha Amitābha (Amida)
**Pure Land Sūtras**   Mahāyāna scriptures dealing with the Pure Land

**Rinzai**   a Japanese version of the Meditation school (Zen) founded by Eisai (1141–1215 CE)
**Risshō Kōseikai**   a modern version of Nichiren's teaching
**rūpa**   form
**rūpa kāya**   form body of the Buddha

**Saicho**   (762–822), founder of the Japanese Tendai school
**sambhoga kāya**   enjoyment body of the Buddha
**saṃjñā**   perception
**saṃsāra**   wandering, process of rebirth
**saṃskāra**   volition, will or impulse
**samudaya**   arising (of unsatisfactoriness or suffering)
**sangha**   community, often used to refer to the community of Buddhist monks (and nuns)
**Sangharakshita**   formerly Dennis Lingwood, founder of the Western Buddhist Order (WBO)
**Śāntarakṣita**   an Indian Buddhist missionary to Tibet who started the building of the Samye monastery
**Sarvāstivāda**   an early school of Buddhism
**shakubuku**   'breaking and subduing', a technique for converting people used by the Nichiren schools of Japan
**Shinran**   (1173–1263), founder of the Japanese Jōdo Shinshū (True Pure Land) school
**Shintō**   native Japanese religion
**Shōmu**   Japanese ruler from 724 to 749 CE, a great supporter of Buddhism

**Shōtoku**   Japanese ruler from 592 to 621 CE, a great supporter of Buddhism
**siddha**   'perfected one', a Tantric saint
**Siddhārtha Gautama**   the Buddha's personal name
**skhandha**   bundle, component of person
**Sōka Gakkai**   a modern version of Nichiren's teachings
**Son**   Korean version of the Meditation school (Ch'an/Zen)
**Sōto**   a Japanese version of the Meditation school (Zen), founded by Dōgen (1200–53 CE)
**Sthavira (Thera)**   elder
**Sthaviravāda (Theravāda)**   the Way of the Elders, a school of Buddhism
**Śuddhodana**   the Buddha's father
**śūnyatā**   emptiness
**Sūtra Piṭaka**   basket of discourses

**Taoism**   the philosophy of the Way (Chinese)
**Tenjur**   Tibetan Buddhist scriptures attributed to famous Buddhist teachers
**Theravāda**   *see* Sthaviravāda
**Thien**   Vietnamese version of the Meditation school (Ch'an/Zen)
**T'ien-t'ai**   a Chinese Mahāyāna school
**tripiṭaka**   three baskets (collections of scriptures)
**Tsong Khapa**   (1357–1419), founder of the Gelug school of Tibetan Buddhism
**Tuṣita Heaven**   a place where *buddhas*-to-be are born immediately before their final birth, a very good place to be reborn

**Udraka Rāmaputra**   one of the Buddha's meditation teachers

**Vairocana**   one of the cosmic *buddhas*, a huge bronze statue of Vairocana is situated in the Todaji temple at Nara, Japan
**Vaiśakha (Wesak)**   Theravāda festival celebrating the Buddha's birth, enlightenment and death
**vajra ācarya**   'diamond teacher', Nepalese Tantric teacher
**vedanā**   feeling, sensation
**vihāra**   monastery
**vijñāna**   consciousness
**Vinaya Piṭaka**   basket of monastic rules
**Vīpassin**   a *buddha* before Siddhartha

**Yaśas**   the Buddha's sixth convert
**Yogācāra**   'yoga practice', a philosophical school of Mahāyāna Buddhism

**zazen**   'just sitting' meditation
**Zen**   the Meditation school, Japanese Mahāyāna

# *Index*